Selected Poems

GERALDINE MONK was born in Blackburn, Lancashire in 1952. Via a variety of routes and circumstances she came to Sheffield, South Yorkshire in 1984. She has lived there ever since.

Selected Poems

Geraldine Monk

SALT

PUBLISHED BY SALT PUBLISHING
PO Box 937, Great Wilbraham PDO, Cambridge CB1 5JX United Kingdom
PO Box 202, Applecross, Western Australia 6153

All rights reserved

© Geraldine Monk, 2003

The right of Geraldine Monk to be identified as the
author of this work has been asserted by her in accordance
with Section 77 of the Copyright, Designs and Patents Act 1988.

This book is in copyright. Subject to statutory exception
and to provisions of relevant collective licensing agreements,
no reproduction of any part may take place without the written
permission of Salt Publishing.

First published 2003

Printed and bound in the United Kingdom by Lightning Source

Typeset in Swift 9.5 / 13

*This book is sold subject to the conditions that it shall not,
by way of trade or otherwise, be lent, re-sold, hired out,
or otherwise circulated without the publisher's prior consent
in any form of binding or cover other than that in which
it is published and without a similar condition including this
condition being imposed on the subsequent purchaser.*

ISBN 1 876857 69 2 paperback

SP

1 3 5 7 9 8 6 4 2

For my darling Alan

Contents

Long Wake	1
Rotations	11
La Quinta del Sordo	17
Banquet	25
Angles Diversions Corners	31
Animal Crackers	43
Sky Scrapers	51
Herein Lie Tales of Two Inner Cities	75
Latitudes	85
Interregnum	97
Trilogy	165
Manufractured Moon	185
The Transparent Ones	195
Insubstantial Thoughts on the Transubstantiation of the Text.	213
Absent Friends	227
Notes	235

Acknowledgments

The longer sequences of poems collected here are reprinted in their original forms with the exception of *Herein Lie Tales of Two Inner Cities* which has been radically reworked and edited.

Long Wake. Writers Forum/Pirate Press, 1979.
Rotations. Siren Press, 1979.
La Quinta del Sordo. Writers Forum, 1980.
Banquet. Siren Press, 1980.
Angles/Diversions/Corners (Tiger Lilies). Rivelin Press, 1982.
Animal Crackers. Writers Forum, 1984.
Sky Scrapers. Galloping Dog Press, 1986.
Herein Lie Tales of Two Inner Cities. Writers Forum, 1988.
Latitudes (from *Quaquaversals*). Writer Forum, 1990.
Interregnum. Creation Books, 1994.
Trilogy. Gargoyle Editions, 2000.
Manufractured Moon and *The Transparent Ones* (from *Noctivagations*).
    West House Books, 2001.
Insubstantial Thoughts. West House Books & The Paper, 2002 .
Absent Friends. Gargoyle Editions, 2002.

A shorter selection including some of these poems was published by North & South in 1992 under the title *The Sway of Precious Demons.*

Also a big thank you to all the magazines and anthologies who have published my work over years.

Long Wake

Beacon Hill – *The Coming of the Night*

Settlement   Settling
      instinctive navigations
      to the final procession

Flicking days off   Picking words from
our lives like   between our teeth
cornflies   sweet spiky apples
                                        Hograh

```
          HOGRAH        SILPHO
              STUDFAST HILL
        JUGGER HOW    SCALING DAM
                 LASKILL
                A         A
                D         S
                S         T
                K         K
                I         I
                L         L
            L   A   D   K   I   L
```

                This is night

Ma-ni-na-le-ha-no   Let it fly —— the arrow
Ma-ni-na-le-ha-no   Let it fly —— the arrow

Hin-khu lush-ka-le   Let me loose I cry
Hin-khu lush-ka-le   Let me loose I cry

'The hooded hawk' my little cock sparrow 'The hooded hawk'

                This is night

Dream One *** Missiles

Here stands my / Father and / I on thesea / shore /
watching thou / sands of / silver / fish uniform /
precision / polaris / missiles leaping / bring / ing
storm / cloudcreep / ing horizon / solitary /
Sea vanishes. . . . arrival. . . . army. . . . plastic bags. . . .
stranded fish. . . . camouflagedfoliage. . . . no. . . . sense of. . . .
occasion. . . . creeping. . . . taking them away. . . . stranded fish. . . .
in plastic bags. . . .

Dream Two***Corridor

Squares black white
black white surroun
D unrelen T jumped
and rolled through
eyes pulsate flicke
red grew isotropic
desolation not tech
nicoloured carnival
black white T.V.O.K.
no two three one fa
ncy dress not givin
g prizes for elepha
feet slap and echoe
s tunnel wet sounds
plash ALONE drips i
n front who behind
find no go or one t
wo tidy shadowy orn
eat figure ALONE co
ncrete in this whit
e black and
corridor

Stump Cross – *The Long Wait*

Stone Ruck   a place   tired pinnacle?

Tired People   a person   my grandmother?

        I was six perhaps seven
        She was bone china eggshell
        lying amongst candles and flowers
        She was wild cold bryonies
        I smiled
        She was only beautiful

Worm Sike Rigg   a place   for dead?

The Dead   a person   my grandmother?

Nakahu-kahu   go to sleep

Nakahu-kahu   go to sleep

Return of Dream One***Pendulum

The fish are / dead / lying open / mouthed / I / walk
village / streetdown / towards / deathwake / cure I /
have / biscuits soaked in lemon / juicesky sea / at
mostphere lem / onjuice / the fish / willwake / willmake /
lively as Scaling / Dam in Spring /
Above.... lemon.... skyjuice.... swings.... silently....
suspended.... a pendulum.... the time.... struggles....
it is.... I think....

Return of Dream Two***Corridor

Emerging me and little seconds turned monsters of time and consequen cellophane wrapped a packed scream of **d e l i g h t** my sugar da ng erous need you insulin poly und satur-day sport with grand standard have you jig-a-jig-jog ing your carbon monoxide dead beat feet back down the black and white white black and corridor

The Three Tremblers – *The Coming of the Dawn*

Spirits submerged form frantic quivers

Are you three hills
    three days without moon
    three opposite faces expertly contrived

Have you upturned relics and grey matter centres
    projecting   waves
    of broad sounds   moving sea snakes

Do vibrating liquids flood Miley Pike or Bloody Beck when you
    wake?

Perhaps three hours before dawn or
    the one before
    the one   tween
    the one   hind or after the threatening sun

When we pass you today
    will we tremble
    will our backchat curdle

Return of Dream One***Protrusion

Aroom immense / amidsummer / mourning / the passing /
equilibrium / aroom that / containsacertain / encroachment /
seaswelliN/Sidious / rise and / rise and / noebbflow /
rise and / further no / abatement /
Aroom minute.... abed.... roomdream.... disturbed....
walls.... cave... crack... protrusion... appears...
hideous... haggaback.... fatlipped.... Leviathan....

Return of Dream Two***Corridor

Claustrophobic silos
of compressed homo s
ap down you running
concrete blood small
mono mole holes an i
sotropic nightmare o
f probabilities no F
issile gag no laugh
your breaking pressu
re point snapping cr
ackled and split us
spitting white and black
and
corridor

Lyke Wake – *The Coming of the Snow*

                        Bury my heart
Upon the night   Upon the night
                     settling like
                     a death moth
         white knots   drift

    and fleet   and candle light
                           on
                      Fire Tower

          If ever thou   meat or drink
          fire or shrink   meat or drink
          If ever not known
          fire or bone   meet the Brig o' Dread

Ice is breaking   t a b e g i l o k

Ice is breaking   t a b e g i l o k

Hey-ye hey-ye   hey-ye hey-ye
Clasp my hand and part   nape-mayuza
                     Bury my heart
phosphorus   snow ghost

        passing strangely now
        feline shivers of
        violet and blue ignite
                  caress this mute
                            albino.

Rotations

Spring

Plucking scales and callouses
off February days
finds Spring shy and reluctant
to show young nipples
whilst Sirius and Orion
still voyeur

The brittle morning air
soaked in vinegar cracked
with wing
beats and mating
cries

The tenuous air swelling
body heat
excitement
      Brides Spring from oblivion
      to provincial newspapers
           only child of carried pos y ounger sister
           brothermother crepe and chiffon
           best ma n erves fumb/rin
           gand champagne comes now shooting
                              messages
                                suggestions

    Its easy you see
    these green and white fluids
    ferreting through stems & hollows

        exquisite propulsion

      swallowing emptinessess — bringing
salt to tongue tip song
for this sticky season

Summer

Inertia sweats from pores
                         out
under cyanosed skies
merging
attic heat bitch and dog
rose — red-nosed judges

Sea weary of clockwork
and moonpull
juggles electric
storms and day-trippers
with a little time

and time again this
endless circuit gathers —
rose thorns — temple teeth
spiky and speakeasy
the she-devil Cassiopeia
                         W zips rip and
                         M's
                suspicious
veins on
air veins of damsel
flies down your forehead
a shiver of blue
heated twilight

Autumn

This brief hiatus
between Summer and Winter
filled with mounds
of sodden kid skin   mottled
  with spicy putrefaction

Fungi perfect their spores gorge
sardonic emulations
stealing the essence
of almonds and
slaughter houses
        leaves impressions

                      'Somebody's got to clean
Moonglobe cannonball   the bloody things up'
cochineal rises   council workmen keeling
towards Andromeda   as escaped nature goes on the
                                          rampage
                      vandalising tar-macadam

        remains

Autumn's half-closed
eyes of lovers
swamped in the arms of
Little Death

Winter

Beneath the Pleiades
days are coated in tar and fibre-glass
lovers roll from warm sheets to desolation
spearing shards
              c-old
                      separation
growing stale-eyed as the sun

Canine mouth dripping icicles
tongue licking cheeks neat
whiskey raw &
burning   sweetmeats
      white flash
feet   fleshing
                    bedroom floor.

Winter stalking
black wolf pelts rain
and caustic winds
                    carries the coffin/kills
                    holds the baby over the hills
                    away away he paws away
                    at this most derelict season

La Quinta del Sordo

La Quinta del Sordo

Did they begin with
a sharp and a parched rasp
                              a hissling furnace
a gang of heckling menace

Did they come sooner or
sooner still
            filtering through
goose kicking or belly snaking
with lobster arms and side stepping shadows

And they became yours all yours
sweet and sticky leeches of twilight
begging always and all ways with
slanted faces

a nerve instance — threadbare
            cold meat torsos

They needed you
They kneaded you — exclusively

these draped men and dripping soldiers
these poor and animal antics
performing and consuming

How tight grew your creatures of myth
How tight grew the monkey wrench

1

lunar masque

an equine head rears	a woman's face bleeds white
prehensile lips	before ruin
bloodsucking and hooked in	two black trenches
rapacious horse play	crush down on cheekbones
created and swollen	charcoal on chalk
with frenzy	choking black ivy

stricken
seaquake
of
iron limbs
overwrought
straddle
airquake
and beyond
the aftermath
unblinking
the eye of a squid
devours
their future shadows
stretched and melted wax
frozen
partners in fatigue
seething
webbed and fossilized exhaustion

2

We are gathered here today
because peacocks are pretty birds
and perfect monsters of iridescence
Moreover the world has stumbled and tumbled viciously
off its floating circles and finally concussed under
timid speech
We shall begin to wail (sostenuto) with ill will and abundance
Yes we have alighted here today keen and clever
on the fallen margins of space and
unchangeable germ-plasms
knowing why colours crack with moods and moving lips
and telling no secrets of the bagged and sonic chieftains
So all is safely gathered thin and perishing
on its devious route to death
but we will not follow such wandering disasters
we are too smug and swinging
happy from this bough and bony thing

3

You will go where I go where I and you go twinning
this Siamese disease forming bunches of limbs
fused in trepidation

You remain me and I and you with these taunting
ligatures of skin binding mutual
assailants

Inextricable

we are
compulsory chaperones
a nexus of stretching
nerve
drained currents and
overheated desires

squabbling before
this obese gutter pressing crowd
this strata galvanised and quickened to animosity
to a baby old chick head revving up squawks to lasso
our hideous display

And here more hooks more eyes and this
fleshless wet bandaging of loneliness with black marrow gape

Come now
Let us beckon
Let us reckon hard
with this block vengeance

4

Here we go sound around the one in the middle who we
shall riddle   the bulbous head pearing away we're
laughing at you   clenched fists may pray and black
out night to fight the   heardings   AMPLIFICATIONS
go sound around and   jutters through shutters and   B
rained stained cellars   now you are the queen who'll
never be seen you're   one on your own so far   from
home a pig in a choke/spoke more kindly of/a spoke   in
the eye/s ticks bent will flick and pick up the pieces
of shadows we form for your   ultimate   annoyance
so turn a blind/find/d eye look find/ers are keep/ers
and we are yours but   it's only some fun so don't run
for a while just tow the line and you'll be   perhaps
and maybe wet with sweet dew if the morning ever   or
never

                    5
        sabres topple HUNCH THAT knocks on fever
                 low BELLOWING shroud
        hitting that largest MUSCLE shunting bloodrowned
              crumpling at THE slightest shade
                       UNKNOWN
                         THE
                        HEART
              breaking fierce A wishing bone
                  THICKENING PEWTER
                        HUSK A
                         DRUM
              sound BRITTLE WEAPON gargles
                       DILATING
                         AND
                    CRISS A CROSS
                        NAILS
                          SH
           IMSHI   OUT   IMSHI
                        IMSHI

Banquet

        S U N balanced

            pivotal

      swung overhang and

       setting warm then

          westwith

       the red and seedy

        EXTRAVAGANCE

        of pomegranates

            *

The nucleus is threatened
chiaroscuro beautifying horror
skittish with a corner glance
the peacock loudly called
(from gilded beak)
ILLUME pole star
turn ruby curls
turn wine to darker gems/stemmed
and tapered
for this sad banquet

            *

Eating bread and honey Queen
                hair spiked and fanning
torments
of the four and twenty
done to a turn —— surreptitiously
the deck of cards collapsed
g
  l
    i
      s
        s
          a
            n
              d
                o
to the ace of death
whilst O.K. Jack Winkle
(twinkling little perisher)

laughed up his embroidered sleeve

*

—— the peacock loudly called
BURY the hatching
WILD ——
deep in shrill eyed
losers
hawking doves & demons —
horns apart — detecting?

eidetic breeze strokes exile — beguiling —

*

    the infatuation with strangeness
    the fragrance   SATURNine intoxication
    submerged by
    oceanscenting light
    waves   dreams   green in black
    olivenite   chartreuse
    and the soft spot
            light blushing rouge
                        to vivification
    succulence on the gentle push
                    to putrefaction
            festivities grow superstitious

*

    Orb into Dome into
    quizzical illusion
—— egg ellipsing ——
    advocaat on hazels for the
    cool tooth of nugget ——
    seismic contraband
    thrown
    PLOSIVE
    from gilded beak

*

JUST
a moment to
    pick up the threading
    mosses-come-galaxies
    come crunch and spongy
        a moment so
            NESTSOFT and neon gas-p-lashes
           PEACH so gentle bruised GINGER
                              flames
          BRANDY   swelling
            CHERRIES   cerise
a moment for
    the carving knife — manicured — precipitating —

                *

    Through arched-back windows
    high
    spitting leuco-livid dawn
    on same coloured neck
    tickled by blood beads/love
    beads
    lull lull
    of seduction —
    muted echo of sibilations
    (small delicacies of brilliance)

Angles Diversions Corners

A

thisa one
off a
shoot at
angles
from side
to zenith to
down deep-
estRange
about t
urns cork
screw a
gain ca
tch wind
ow
frame re
flect f
lick knife
points
of
glasshine
glint re
BOUND to
RE
    gret

c
reased up
slang
matching
di
sect of
word
playing
Time by
ear
mouthing

barb-s-
piccato
spin rift
    drift
wonder
relics
from spine
up star de
lux to
astrocyte

RUSE
ruse ab
 use
ing voltage
for fun &
game
changing
part
ners two two
timing paso
doble
automated
interrupt
of cadence over
and out
OUT now
symbiont
precision

con
volutions
spiral gyro
scope of
much
and more

behind
the breach that
thought that
nought that
note so
final
B flat B
nothing
O B Just
joy riding
out on limb an'
thanat-an-atom
    E an-
        atomical
to infin
con
   brio

D

eight dead
(words)
follow eight
bizarre

shapes thicken on Q
U q wavering back
to black
backtoback
dis
   joint
ramblings
       loners
escap
    es
      capade
twelve frayed
letters
more dull words sip
tea
   flip
records
accounts
      money or
disturbance broke
bout of
drink
port
gin sucked
grim
inability

(on the rocks)

duelde-
ception

just 'cause
just
cause effect
neglect
accidental fall
to squalor and
rosebay will

       follow
DI
versions go
slow
slow
quick quick
go
hunting violets
and money mad
at the door
more sawdust for
your heavy lust
not known
try next but one
THING
take your foot
off my floor
polished
to reflect
heaven

hard

core

pared

separate

carve

d

ou

T

crushed
attitude of
dawn
pearls your
skin
copper
tin
aluminium
thin
moon metal
      gun
smoke
      coils
disturbance broke
duelde-
ception

eight dead

hunting violets

C

mea cul
PA see
brave mama
don't know
what
HIT or
came
from dark
     shot at
       turn
instan
TrembL
ull
tremba
gain
whywhi
chway
to turn
out corners
loose ends
mend

the other
D
ay No
great thing
it is
FOR

bidden
to talk
about the

hhhrt

about

the
HEART   fling
to
future
YES
think
bleak
ly LY
ing B
lacking
ebon

sericeous
half light
heart to
half
SUB
merge
switch back
full
on di
STurb
web and
fascinate

light blue
then stand
well
back
aligned
with
remote
ness
control
ThisThat
star and

kiss bye
by the wayside
kiss sugar
stealers sneak
thieving
moisture pearls

nuzzle
purpose of
all
grieving
wet or
high
dry
chuckle
death
ly und er
fing er
tips flow
er blade
steal to softly
senses
took leave
of
the other
    other
day
NO

re
currence
less
exhilarates
s

Animal Crackers

Dragon   Fly   Howling   Monkey

softly   softly
lacepale
rustlings basically what
you get in skeletons this
side of hell
        fragmented
                  smoke/croak of internal roughness
      begging for movement
accommodating dance bands
so apt so
go-go so
      phobic contortions fly &
      howl agro-
             vating bottle-
                  neck wrapping chatter
                  flap a
                  flap

Honey   Bee   Soldier   Beetle

zero latitude for love
sunsnivels/miserably needling
for relief
Comic cutting retinue
straining wick and
sucking/up glory bruised/with
burden-churning
sweet-meats for
others

Fruit　　Bat　　Cake　　Urchin

bitten clean in
two　　　　ill
　　divided
　　feasts

mythical swoop
folding up
on passion –
teeth –　what for?

Glass　　Snake　　Electric　　Eel

mirror voltage/watery
　　sh/ock manically
　　　　　gathering face
　　　　　muscles /freeze
　　　　　in sp/l/it
　　　　　　　Eternity
shedding
　　　past
glider
　　　undergrowth
softly trickle
hiss and
shimmy

Blister   Beetle   Polar   Bear

oily burst north/
wards arctic pressing
equator
non-a-voiding uproar
tea/green and gin
flowing apace
ooze/
hugging to/deadlock slide/easy on/
devastation

Umbrella   Bird   Snowy   Owl

hooded cyphers
reverse of hoax
wild surges in chiaroscuro
wing dripped from below
tip disappearing
vibrancy
driven to fascinate

Hellbender   Salamander   Mountain   Lion

caustic
slither of
night/deadly tangent a
                    wrong path the
                    only path
chiselled
        sleek
            whisperings   aside
                    Vile
                        clichéd
                Seducers

Ghost   Crab   Seed   Shrimp

greenish crawl marine
buds through
        strange
        season feeling for
other/
ness transX lucidity
veering on sinister and
ridicule

incipient & vanished impressions
rooting limbless
sub-haunted mind/mid
day traffic can
not
Drown

Earth   Pig   Sun   Spider

crashing awkwardly spiked
                         drink
             on
soft fruit
cocktail gold/of
             blood turns/of
                         lemon
Desires from overlapping
spinning pink and messy
opposites colliding

Rainbow   Boa   Butcher   Bird

uneasy embrace grows
getting
constricted
thrown on slab/back
breaking
spit
   gushing
arch reds to indigo
feathered and bled

Sky Scrapers

CI

Cirrus
high
ice
crystals splitter-zip to
neatly razored
fixed shape

lacking shadow
lacking water experience or
inclination or hunch of rushes
lush bathers   sea storms
LIBATIONS

high
detached delico
whitey appearance
feather tread – ghost frisson
rising slowly

rising slowly
first crack of / cigarette
smoke detaching
delico drew
unresolved patches
assuming filaments
whispery white now
rising slowly above blankets
lingering high behind curtains
clouding ornamental glass
                       light

shade on upper
coming on from South West

approaching depression
hours even
days   days   days   away

behind

infinity somewhat relaxed

Today
sky vital   frenetic

early morning   ice-angulated sun
skids too brightly cross
capsized energy unready
for day crystals
                fruit scowls
lemon   lemon
                rue then brittle
apples and antlers

the reluctance and flounderings
dried fish in porcelain
globe in loveless space

CC

Cirrocumulus
you know it
elemental grains
merge to separate
dribbling
splints of herring bone
mackerel glints   ripply
rounders
pebbly corrugations
connotations ripe with pure rustic
clusters
quaint as quangos
                clusters abruptly cancelled
                by first flick and docking
                roughly in vicinity of
                ashtray
                first abrupt numbing and
                rallying of body swerves
                slow uncurl of backbone
                stretching for ritual hunt of
                lost imperatives
the first splintering
from fine to unsettled

indicative of change

sweet relief

Today
sky provocative   skittish

this season is forward
energy coming as blackbird
unlimited humour
larks and others
arrange wreaths furtively

in background
slight levitations

after gales in forest   shut and
shadow fall
came raps of tenderness

light colouring matter

CS

Cirrostratus
smooth   subdued
still kinda whitish
but veiled
        partially
sometimes   or   sometimes
           totally

transparent overcast
breeding
kinda whitish rimmed
haloes
spiralling down to
consumptive rouge
with   bits   of   seethe   and   brood
very low keyed rage

another step in depression sequence

last and empty pkt under footcrush

approaching rain
promising small insects walkies
on water

Today
sky vacant   prosaic

after drenching and departures

almost carved in a tree
'we're out of control' —
cold tea and a quick meal disastrously
decorates book cover

(smears of crime move with wild-fire spread)

puzzles testing resilience to facts
keeping out fear
                    rudimentary horns may
sprout from rocks

(theatrics breaking out of bounds)

almost wrote on the wall
'we're straining the day out'

AC

Altocumulus
bragging shadow plus
big scaled
thickness

white bowing out now
                            reluctant
haloes
invert to coronas
                coral rimmed
eyes sting on smoke and
light wave
        trigger
of greenness
impressing many dreams touched
sour
aristocratically hung till
maggoty
or more commonly till
hungering layers
of shading weighs humourless
rolling memories / cigarettes / clouds
which may / may not

be merged

Today
sky vanity charged muscular

the ritual cuppa
the rare spit-polished apple

peaches and dreams

on entering the dance backwards
a fierce storm was drenching
getting up
not being contained
getting snarled in weeds
lash
fins
slithery

from an early age
blows rendered powerless
with even bits of magic
holding in a sob

destroyer where middle of ocean should be

AS

Altostratus
impoverished
dull   sheet   layer
thin enough
grey enough
babycham without
brandy

approaching wet
may even pour
may even enough to
soak watery moon disc
of sun
OUT

thinking how a giant
gestural skid mark of
cerulean blue or
jigger of red rum would
break it nicely
          how a jiggle and a zig-zag cockles
          innocence to treachery
          sends old familiar
          stampeding

sinister how weather determines mood

sinister how right on cue
clouds and smoke thicken
enough

Today
sky rheumy   congealed

on turning we saw the very scene we dreaded

space curled up

applause for legends

ebbing tides and silt

earth keeping love in check

SC

    Stratocumulus   Romulus
                Remus
     low   lumpy rollings
             indicating

          NOTHING

Today
sky puzzled   lumpy

a party kept dark

no ray penetrating fine dress fabric
(hugs will crush these gowns and
ornaments rigged up with precision)

complexions take a knock looking sullen
bruised   dreadfully dark

trouble that could be threat

water rats departing with the old comedian old
judge turning off-sage green his
tongue going into beer thrillingly

'cream bun, dear?'

leggy birds gathering on the water edge
smoke rings gathering on the water edge
moderation leaving Mr. Loudmouth in one
recurring speech disease

energy kept in by a lid

ST

Stratus
off-ground fog   low rush
hush   drizzle
gradual hill wash out
gradual uniformity
ragged patches –
take your pick
at direction

slow drag and shove of voices
rolling low on memory wind

take your pick at direction
                past looping push
                pull luscious
                sounds
                betraying spiked nervy actions
drag and shove of
sublunary crooners staggering
space after 'time'

discernible outlines
no haloes though no
blue up above everyone in
lovey-dovey lazy river happy
just a
once forgotten love stub / another
cigarette
ragged patches

Today
sky uncomfortable   hunched condition

bird circling   arrives in tree
gentle disturbance

desire making you pale
twisted
about to be late

yes, in a way
happiness ebbing within

little energy for depravity

the point is
to accept mood merrily

NS

Nimbostratus
watery low
pressing
rain
eternal
    like last
        vast and black middlenight how
        many hours till dawn
        alone feel
        time cessation
        when all who loveyou
        youlove sleep –
        weightwater flood river
        fish occasional moon boulders
        half flowers curled back sepals
        weeping fingertips in creamcool dip
        licked luxuriously slow
no gap emerging
between sky and
sea shooting breeze
and livid
moods

just and endless drag
with no deep sighs

Today
sky overturned   annoyed

layers of unclearness must be removed

the sidetracking of the quest
stopping right here with
rough sea in a language
that comes full of wriggles and
special charm

CU

Cumulus
ambiguous
timid   portentous   wild
high rise of convoluted domes
d r i f t i n g   s l o w l y

soft vertical brilliances
grafted on dark
horizontal bluntness

silent carriers
travelling through contradictions
smiles riding sibilations

a desire salted / compressed
a compulsion without pressure
vivacity leaning on death wish

insidious avalanches

Today
sky nerve crested   fragile
clouded craven dawns to
exaggerations of declamatory sunsets

elaborate farewells

it's a trick

love turning chapters
trailing love in power

beat not heart –
excessively

CB

Cumulonimbus
umbras

slow   creep   of   megatons

tainted expanses
sickly pink

jaundiced
                       dense thickened milk/
                       memory siege
                       touches from past
                       the thin almost non/
                       existent taste of beer
                       emphasising attraction/
                       repulsion accepting a
                       kiss or
                       withdrawing
slow
creep
of
megatons

over
powering

Sforzando

Today
sky brutal   arctic

bull struck madly
(middle-section-coming-out)
falling heroes

brawls   card games
    flutters & docking
ship flowers salted petals

wildcat hearts race rudely

supporter had trouble containing volume
he swaggered afternoon earth
scorched by haste over fag ends

one rambling rosette

Herein Lie Tales of Two Inner Cities

Who are
the trespassers?

    Macro-Vulgar-

Macro-vulgar-cosmic
space to rubik cube
contriving relativity
within four walls
beyond all jolly japes
all spies with bidet eyes
    wanting words and
    stale squared equations....
        Barely Moving
barely
moving / stratus formed un /
formed / liquid b / linking
off-side thinker
unsurety
add / itional endure
    hence
      the leaving of
      grieving of
    last
      day emberglow
    hitting all time
    bottomless
    out-adepth
        Freedom
freedom
of info?
Who're kidding kid?
Me? Perhaps not
my shadow
gliding down elevators
hey! there be-bop

grape-quash
all out Baccy
(knowhaddamean)
nota winda left to clean
on Para Street

                                      Another
another step back
breaks
precipitous nightmare
gosht
heaves a certain
curtain certain
          ly want of lambkin solace
               t'deaden definitions
        once removed
              remoteness in
      control
              soundshufts to
      futilities
             descriptive facilities
              animal
            cri de Coeur

                                      Exhilaration
exhilaration of spring day
twisted dark
it's a lark
a high flying jitter-
spraying menace
LIES outs' of speech
LIES outs' of reason
LIES right
down to that
common denom-

inator atoms-a-stom-
ache heaving
charred
flack
humour . . .
            Glads

Glads
  no open
no bloom
    no scarlet finale
blackflying feasters
sapped you flourish
no slow unfurl
creepy un
cur
ling length
ways —
such a suchness
when all else
perfected. . . .
            Without

without recipe
tin man spinning no
perfumes which start affairs
no mischief of sudden growth no
no mans land on
spoils of
war
spoils of non-possessed
place pale and sickly
limit
snow blinded storm

'There is no space only kilometres'
            Elements

elements arguing

oxygen need
to breathe in
to burn
time turning tide
waits for no inefficiency -
Sun too
how deranged
this
precision

                                                          Defiant

Defiant morning
glories
radiate languid beauty to
to nothing and
Nagasaki

Rare terrified humours
linger
suggest solar eclipse stop
war drama

Chill disturbance of hieroglyphs
'I have seen yesterday
I know tomorrow'

A line from Yeats
'Irrational streams of blood are staining earth'

                                                             Rain

Rain sax
ophonic   sycamores
drift
hitching siren
softly uppers to
cres

```
cendo
    rose
runner
    hot
red sum
and total
best of both
turn
    over
snaking
    ladders
```

                                                         Prevail

```
Prevail!
Democracy will
in Death all things
better than
        Red
only
        Injun
        dead
        heat
it's a good 'un
```

                                                        Power

```
Power heat
edging sterility
instantaneous decay
                grizzled / yellowish metals
chill

is there an Aztec
in the house?

sacrifice
calling . . .
```

Glass

Glass-shatter crept anti-
'long shushnow dark waveries
upstaging
      masqueraders
dis . . . . everything
    AH
  unfunny
melotraumatics
   OH
life's little thespians

Transgression of Hemispheres

Transgression of
Hemispheres

Epilogue

So we were clapped in irons
after chewing up roots
extremely neat
stirring salts in water
removing hostile measures
extremely right
but tell on
        What body in equilibrium sums clockwise?
downsloper
        inspecting flagstones
volcanic origins
looking for shade
looking for pillowy plush
        (Re-issuing of hearts)

going round drink
happened a wounded animal
ruthless mood in angrr
raised hair of cattish
        back cunning trick
an over sight of distress
        (Fish hooking the None Seekers)

One tract
One breed of flower
One strained statue locking
        (z) daggers (z)
        What body in equilibrium sums anti?
In scientific space time
    the crime of
evolution
    of visceral clusters
        (Quantum leaps to Obscurity)

claustrophobic dashes
    for
Air   flight   fan   dango

           funfizz
Spume anti-sham Bubbly
                         (Something of the Night)

touched then transgressed
        then rapt stark
stem to eye to sun
a low down show
                         (High Noon)
two rising confrontations
clean obscene
melancholia out to psych
                         (O)
edges moan with depression
                         (Midway Meridians)
the definitive wrong turn
        achieved with ease
archetypal etceteras
        tragic influence
not yet exaggerated

fatally

it seems
violent sorrow seems
a modern ecstasy
                         (Humour poised on Gatecrash)

Latitudes

An Elegy Written in an Unmarked Northern City Graveyard

It is. And it is not. A night in arms. Long.
Flesh. And not flesh. Longing.
Holding high torches positioned recklessly.
From the outskirts to the inner ring. Economic gradations.
Of colour. Shape. Growth.
Allocations of greenery.
The old Oak Tree.

Not just one wounded. Drug for circulation
requiring time to intercept the breakdown with
needle point precision.
(We do not reward the lioness in action.
 We do not decorate the cunning den. Or.
  Applaud stalking. Or. Guerrilla tactics.)

It is still night. It is moving. Changing.
Still. Holly. Holly. Holly.
Evergreen.

Above. And.   Below the crazed cracked flags the
              inn signs swayed as is their wont in all
              tales of ghostiness and shadowy.
              Swayed. Wind-butted. Beaten. Thin. Hollow.
              Bruised emblems. But here the dawn only
              breaks through emblems. Breaks. Yes.
              But how! Rig dyke rising. Flying childers.
              Ark. Angel. Apollo.
              Dove.
              Moonraker.
              Yew tree.

But there are others.
The cross. of.
        Guns. Scythes. Daggers.
The anger.

The cruciform.
The rich red seepage.
Cherry Tree.

A Eulogy Written in an Unmarked Northern City Pub

It is night. Or. It is day. It is timeless.
Sporadic fighting breaks. Is quickly quelled.
All things considered. Proximity excites. Generating passion.
Desirability. To have contact. To consume. To drink deep.
Long. Soft. Hard. Break and.
Soak.
Bread.

Green light from shaded pool. Tables of time without tide.
The lilt of tower blocks with awakenings in the sky or
hibernations entrenched in basement undergrowths.
Rarely at street level. Few wise. Most nibble and peck.
Nuts.
Seeds.

It is see-saw-jig-saw.
        Endless pieces. Parties of choice. And much.
        Wet squelch littered. Concrete. Jolly kiss o' life.
        Painted paddock. Balls. Bells. Tail backs. Feathers.
        Dashes. Exhausts. Upside. Turnaround. Roundabout.
Let's take away.
Buttercross.
Hot fried fishes.

It is still night. It is still day. It is moving. Timeless.
The traffic.
The cues.
The ebb and flow and chink of glasses.
The spills.
The queues.

All jam. All runny.
Cherry cake.

North Bound : Facing South

Alchemical minds turn
cold boreal winters to molten
gold and
all
roads flanked with
hedgerows and horses – swish and
rush and
giddy curves of thatch.
Dumbswept. Vibrant. Earth-hug.

The rich nudge.

The lick of Eden.

Dangerous magic.

Still: one unbroken
flag
not to break our
necks
on would be a
treat
in the rickety
city.

Just to find
one
wild
iris.

North

On this side.
A divide and cast of vowels made to swear
    to shadow the most gentle words.
Even love is flung
    gathering in the throat's pit
a stomach's empty growl.

(Don't 'luv' me cock)

The spirit roosters call and
    spread throughout the night.
Scratching dawn – morning hardly breaks.
    It ups and slithers.

The cock
s
spent up.

The hen
s
well
b
oiled.

Egg.

South Bound : Facing North

Out of tube and tune
buskers   riff
rolling would-be saints and
                soldiers sweat.
(Stiff and prickly's the smell of it)

Such warmth is uncouth.
Such warmth leads to
    sibilants –
the thick hiss and prodding fingers
of sun and subways
               long
    and burn for damp bronchial skies.

Listen: on the downwind
       wheezing amphibians
     full   fuff   fuff
wet-glass-hoppers
crawl and cluck
       cluck opinions
from flat and misspelt eyes
                 panning
and panting
jangled chords of
mischief dealt
fair and tenderly across its
broken bottle landscape.

       Iced
       Glint
       and
       Wink

South

The soured milk and melt of
ju-jubes sluice the jaundiced mind along
to cool shades of yesterday.

Green nostalgia.

You down hills really roll. Smooth.
        Nubile bottoms up and falling. Tipsy.
Your green youth and elders crawl and gang
        with prejudice. From music to misfits.
From A to Z.

Serenade.

Gridded teeth map out.
No Entry. Go Home. Keep Weeping.
Keep walking that mincing
                      step
                            right up
their street
for a short cut.
All narrowness. All fear.

Green Sleeves.

Eulogy in an Unmarked Southern County Graveyard by the Sea

Date to date. A hands span. That is all.
Chiselled print patterns the length of. Innings and out.
Innings and out. Weave. Tangle. Overlap.
Feet deep on a warm summers day.
Skipping tussocks. Stumbling on plots of.
The perfect way to pass
into shade
and breezy.
Kite.

Stone. Of word. Of pared image.
Of cross bones and tricorns.
A grave unsung carver.
With fingers of bone s
              killed in
              tra laa
                      trilling
                            calligraphy.

Skeletal craft. Skimming. Sea lap.
Harbour lips. Rictus. Kiss.
Sucks slowly.
Sucks.
Gulls.

Growth gang. Ging and. Blue chipped. Marble.
Date to date. A hands span. A spirit cheer. Clinks.
Let's fly.
Lark.

Rich one. Poor one. Beggar both. The
opposition to life is
massive and sustained.
Innings and out.
Clock.
Tock.
Cuckoo.

An Elegy in an Unmarked Southern County Pub

So this is England. Blanched. Steeped.
Mouths full of marbles and scratchings.
Speeches full of leftovers.   Full of fag ends. Full of slops.
Served with a face that gives
medicine a lift and
a leg up to
merriment.
Carnival.
Cock.
Chafer.

The snug. The warm sickly draught. Of insularity.
Stagnation. Exclusion. Pick yer winda.
                  Pick any
                          thing
                                to throw and smash the
                                winged and
                                wounded.
                                Dragon.
                                Fly.

Some union Jack. Some bloody union. Remember Jack.
Flying flags. Pigs might. Flies might. Fists might.
No Jack. Not pickets Jack. Don't talk wet. Don't talk
soft Jack.
Jenny.
Wren.
Cherry.
Cake.
Runny.
Oak.
Cricket.

Interregnum

Part 1

Nerve Centre

Pendle

        (brooding dislocation)
          limits
push
    over
iced Pendle water   warm English beer
       sipspeed
        under
    grazing
              headlights
  catch
      odd eye
         startles
hearts
   odd creatures
sometimes missed   sometimes hit
      warm runny things
      cold unmoving tarmac
    (lascivious sprawl   conscious and livid)

The Hill People

GOOD FRIDAY HIKERS

We love to go a-wandering
across this hillside track
with knapsacks filled
with snap
      emergency kits
      Kendal mint cake
on our backs
      Fair Isle sweaters
      Arran
                      (will-we-see the Irish sea
                      beyond Blackpool tower)
Will we see varieties
of heather
recognise cloud formations
insect bites
bird song
      Fol di ree
we fill our lungs
with fresh and windy air
to warble out our
naming of the
parts
      of nature's
rambling
      incoherence
      Fol di raa

Hallowe'en Bikers

blackened cow hides
outride
big roar
night
heavens
hill angels
winging sweet
tassel thrills
skirt
leather sweat out
beer
piss
patchouli
stinking
high-haunch
to hell

studs
ring a-ring
a-rosy
clash a holy
war with
water
air
earth-back
firing up
turned cruci
forms
luring
born-
agains marked &
harking lord laws
peppering
lust through your
crossed-boned
leg-spreading
fundamental
engines

Born Agains

sinlovers
spawning
rubble-rousing
satanic
icons
in the pure woolly
heads of
sheep
eyes
slit
a fester on
your dreams
of thirty
foot
of
stainless steel
erection

on
just a
rather very small
Pennine hill

Pagans

Hail sulphuric eyes
matter-caked orbs
    alignment of baubles
primordial crud
cheapo jewels
seed-stones
planetary pulses
cosmic stew

pure Mother Earth fuck
wet volup of
            Venus
limps off at half-cock
wishy-w
roundandwound
little
circles
pretty patters
clownabout

hula-juggins
rattling prayseeds
gimcrack berry-reds
bead-smear
bloodclots
blossom

DRIVERS

spin
    can
tin   chrome
aluminium womb
fine
    tuned in
  to cruise
        on out
 your
     bloody
MIND
      that ani . . .
              mal
                   (mal)
                       ((mal))

        (((warm runny thing   cold unmoving tarmac)))

Hill Outriders

Shift Workers

I don't stand around
in ones and twos
I stand in
DOZENS
on corners
weaving through
thought
warping
speech
mouth
spelling
contortions pull
and pull clap
bobbin hands over
lips
lick turning
milk
churns sour
in the
middle
I
come
in the night
black
as

JESUIT BOY BLUES

Dear and dogged man. Selfbent, bound;
So tied and turned, brows of such care,
World bare, and none to touch my everywhere
Perfumed, greedy guilt dreams of long-grass
Love-boys, sea-shells, blue-breeze stings and
Salts my tonguing meaty meatless sins to
Whip the words across and cross my precious
Selfworn, world-torn, aching bodybent. Ah!

Fox Hunt

All a sudden all
the people were in out rage and in up roar:
that they fell upon
me knocked me
down and kicked
me trampled me
(and people tumbled over fear)

Led me out and into hands
and 'knock out the teeth of its head' they cried.
So some got hedgestakes and staffs
(and blood ran down several people
as I never saw in my life:
as they was dragging me along)

Dragged me to the common
(moss)
willow rods beat on my head
and arms and back and shoulders
till they mazed me
till I lay a little still
till at
last
I saw myself dying

then staggering and bled
I rose red
a reversed emblem

Fox Trot

weavy	path
	magic quake
	trot
hot	brick
	red
paw	sore
	bluster brain
storm	fit
	shudder limbs
seize	throat
	choke neck-a-neck
	hawk
wise	words
	weep meat
	possessed
meet	moved
	I was moved

I was moved to go up
        to top (IT)
which I did (IT) was so
        very steep and
(HIGH) I was come to top
        (IT) the hill (I)
saw sea to top it the hill
(I) (HIGH) saw (IT) (I)

FLYER

ridge soaring day-late-summer
well-warm valley
moist haze of upcurrent
feathered kind of freedom
ticklish and ho
boning flesh-thought
snapping earth-care to core

    fingers to click
       beat
     flexiwings
      spring
  ridge-life-line and
      upover

(with slamming-surge and stomach-slide
    and expertly a-voiding yaw)

now see the little people-pricks
see their little pin-pricking
steeples to truth
and that motorway-to-nowhere's endless
curb crawling
every curve
in the unlit lights
of day and darker
I
fly across uncontrolled
airspace and
forests

PART 2

Palimpsestus

... perpetual
   dreamdrip-backdrop
   pooling centuries
   deep
   crush and spurt of
   wide-open (or)
   and
   so on
   ting (or)
   jang of nerve chords wend-
   welter.
              quiet ravings of.
   desires.
         fret of sad saltless.   days.
   word-wars.   despair of.
     displacement.   of stagnation.
   (or) bounds of sassy-hugs.
      letter-love.
      daffy-mads.
   beamers and so forth
   so on
   in perpetuity ...

... (STUMBLING SURVIVAL) ...

... giddy with
         it
   sharp
   stumb
   hotmolten

it give:
>   sinew
>   ligament
>   dried mud under painted
>   finger
>   nails chipped red
>   lips
>   tic   grimace
give:
>   raw
>   windfresh
>   cheap little finger-ring
>   glad-stabbed hanging wish
>   boned . . .

. . . **(DISTURBED TRANSFORMATIONS)** . . .

. . . lewd and magical suggestions of
>   form
>   archways of limbs
>   full
>   fungus breathings . . .

. . . **(CORRECTION OF DISFIGUREMENTS)** . . .

. . . Three peaks.
  .Three dream-rollers.
  .Three prickly voices.
   piercing second sight
   chucking up visions from
>   ectoplasmic mists

    unstopped centuries
        seep
    unbearable sorrowlove
        gag
    upon hysterical gag punch
    whole side-splitting
    guts
    get funny-a
    get rot

    such lush lush
    such meretricious bleedings . . .

. . . **(ENTRY ZONE OF HALLUCINATIONS)** . . .

. . . meretricious bleedings
      fruit-dew
     body-bunch
      sex-shiver
fever. fever. fever.

    rotating solar plexus
    bilious beneath stars
    .poisonous butterflies.
    .brooding dislocations.

      a feathered breath
        licks the neck
        .leaves a scar . . .

. . . **(LEGIONS OF FRANTIC MISERIES)** . . .

   . . . so tiny
         drop of fear
   tickles fringe
   of young blood
      wetting scrubbed floorboards
   virginal
      carbolic fist hits
   tiny face-in-waiting
      floods
   bottle-green oceans of
   the world and
   little dog howled
   to see such fun
   such energy-jumps to
   depraved outrage
   and the stained black habit
    flapped away
    cawing
    taa taa taffa-teffy
    taa taa taa-a
    TAA TAA TAFFA-TEFFY
    TAA TAA TAAA-A

      . . . (MIND FULL OF MEAT AND FLOWERS) . . .

      . . . Three aves
        rise
        <small>RISE</small>
        RISE
   (in ascending order)
  hymnal sobtexts gusht
 Fruity Womb and Luv King
    king and queen of
  sacred-obscene-heart

		breaking
		  beat
	pulsating prime time
		EXPOSURE
	hypes meteoric rise of
	Roaring Jack Shirt Ripper
		   aka
		Juice Flasher
	gedda loadda light divine
		lasting longer
		    right
		Your Brightness
		    right
		Roaring Omnipotent
		     O
	Ave and Throbbity Throb
	  goes the grief speaking
		   box . . .

. . . (WAYWARD DELIGHTS) . . .

. . . soft   loonish
   touched   stared
transgressed
waved from wing
then the other
dragged   wide
   dreams   wake
lemonade
shaking fantasy worlds
o
pen
sezza. . . .

. . . (HATCHING PREMONITIONS) . . .

. . . superstitions breeding
  fitful irregularities

    the never-ending shagging of wonderment
    with gentlyness   with defiance   with drollery

    sticking sticky fingers into
    sweet weepings

    passion tides awash un upflood
    to pain-point-hidden-pinks

    bogey man
    mother smell
    witch weavings . . .

. . . (CONTROLLER OF SHADOWS) . . .

. . . Three biters hast thou bitten
  (heart ill eye ill tongue)
  Three bitter fluids mixt
                run
    thickening in
          approaching fear
          approaching drunken storm
          approaching savage same note
          scraping between clenched
                        tooth . . .

. . . (MOUTH DRIPPING VERBAL CRUCIFIXIONS) . . .

. . . Three o clock Good Friday dinner
   hits
       floralwallpaper
   slug
       trail of slowth
   streaks
       wallcrawl to
   oilcloth

   eyes slop about . . .

   redden . . .
   mouth drippens . . .

   dead fish swimming in
   luke-warm vinegar . . .

   sicked-up beer . . .

. . . (GESTURES DESTROYING ALL MEANING) . . .

. . . arise
   make haste
        my love
   my dove
        my beautiful one
   and come
   cum spiritu tuo
   disturbing
        pink
   bedroom landscapes

    fall
        nightlong
    licked clean
    Jack Nazarene and the
        five
    bleeding wounds of passion
    suck
        hushed lily fingers
    love nest . . .

. . . (LASCIVIOUS SPRAWL) . . .

   . . . the old
        suffocating tongue
    giving endless
        so-called kiss
            on
        into the anonymity
    of outer space
           girl
        goes past zone
    of mobility and flux

– withdrawl of logical progressions –

    can't breathe even moan
    girl-mind
           hooks on transference
           out-of-body trance
    crawls into cool dreams of
    future
    disconnected bliss . . .

. . . (PEEPHOLE FROZEN MOANS) . . .

   . . . Three little shit houses
     spawned
     spawned
     spawned
          (NEVER ASKED TO BE)
     spawned
     spawned
     spawned
          (NEVER ASKED TO BE)
     to think
     I
     to think
     I
     to think
     I
     my
     loin seeds
     my me me me
     divided into three
              (NEVER ASKED TO BE)
     little shit houses . . .

. . . (MALICIOUS-ITCH TRANSFERENCE) . . .

...Three women   Three sisters.
                    Three mill workers.
   spin.   wind.   cut.
   FATE.   FATE.   FATE.

                 dispossessed daughters of Eve
                      and Night and
                        all shades
                   ever darken ending
                         spectral
                         shift ...

   ... (FLESHRASP WARNINGS) ...

   ... blinded
      we pinned the tail in
                    the donkey's eye
      brayed
      hilt deep
      mortification

      internal
                      fused con fused
      external

      pule & skirl
      feud & feud
      dubbed on
                      pentatonic
      scales
                      lash

unleash the
lunatic guilt
swings
self into quarry

        haunted hunter . . .

. . . **(HUNTED HAUNTER)** . . .

    . . . flesh fall from
        words
        fade
          to . . .

    . . . **(GHOSTS)** . . .

Part 3

The Great Assembly & Feast

Loped & strungalong the calmquake forests of astonished branches. Crissed rivers teeming spring. Much upona. Clambered hummock and dung and sleeping animal-hill. Ganged Malkin Tower to fest and murder plot. Grow semtex – a likely. Banged up L/caster (via forbid Trough). Run proof. Bolt-stare of stone. S'easy. Blow away – fuft.

Tread flesh & flagstone. Skip cobble nicks. Go dizzy hand-linked rounds. Jitter. Belly knot. Brewst hysterical terror. Turn mindlimbs out their course. Spasmics. Consort then with demons. Drift deep. On rafts of fish skins.

They glamour. They bleed. Deceive. Imperfect animal. Barely once removed from. Come. Snake woman. Wolf woman. Whore woman. Witch. Deformed and depraved mother woman. Worry-to-death woman. Howl all night under reeds. Girlgrace. Blood to nothing. Love seed. Nether smell. Pro terra. Contra mundum.

Spread

                        carved with a penknife

dearly & dangerously

muffled wingbeat of earthslides   Doc Martens

cloggerstomp   devildiscos

liplix

teeth deepin cracked mugger-fingers

                              brace o thief ears

        dog shaped rhubarb   dill pickle & burgers

seacock   blue milk   sparks of salt

              mushrooms of considerable shaping and bigness

atomic tongues

                                    vinegar sponges

assorted skins soaked in moonshine

                  little bone of wolf pizzle

ciborium of pace eggs   arteria magnus of man

wet friday fish   five stone loaves

                      stolen mutton

                    (done to a turn)

and midnight diminished to a sliding oyster

              cruel communions drained

              last sup

                    Innocent's Bull Blood

More than meat or drink. Better than stars and water.
Words birthed. Made flesh. Took wing. Horrids and
enormities. Chantcasters. Daubing lunarscapes.
Stench polluting skies. Broodcasting vile tales. The
abortus embalmed. Babyface on the chopping block.
Death of Our Perpetual Succourpap. Swingalong with
Satan. Donkey cock. Hot crosses. Jack Nazarene and
the Five Bleeding Wounds of Passion sing in a-boo.
Sad-Jack-J in a Waa-Waa. Twisted tales. Tired.
Abominations and filthiest excess. Words took flesh took
flesh. Winged backwards. Shock of hind sight. Foreflight.
Special-speech. Litanies.

Tower room turned. Video shift. Zoom clausto. Hanging
rafters. Meat hooks. Unread omens. Mills about. Satanic.
Dark. Heaving parox. Over come in waves. Passion nudge.
Crushed smiles. Lips slip around stigmatas. Witchmarks.
Wild web. Slip on woman's slippers. Man-made. Thinly
spun man's skin. Lurex. Spindle pricks. Weavers. Spider
rites

Hare spit fire. Green glass gob. Trine. Sextile. Convergence
of Time. Mother winders out your moons. Mashing tea.
Sucklers. Crating hurtables. Webbing exquisites. Gagging
jeers. Flouting magnificence. Slobbering warmth and
familiars. Tib. Dandie. Fancy. Ball. Mock transfixions.
Giving up the. Ghost.

Chantcasters

Demdike Sings

Wild air,
world-mothering air,
nestling me everywhere,
that's fairly mixed
with riddles
and is rife
in every least things life
and nursing element

(Welcome in womb and breast
Birth-milk draw like breath)

Do but stand
where you can lift your hand
skywards;
round four fingergaps
it laps
such sapphire-shot
charged, steeped sky will not
stain light.
                        Mark you this:

It does not prejudice
the glass-blue days
when every colour glows.

Each shape and shadow shows.

The seven or seven times seven
hued sunbeam will transmit.

Perfect.

Not alter it.

Chattox Sings

What we have lighthanded left
will have waked
and have waxed
and have walked
with the wind.
This side,
that side hurling
while we slumbered.
Oh then,
weary then why should we tread?
O why
are we so haggard at the heart,
so care-coiled,
care-killed,
is their no frowning of these wrinkles
ranked wrinkles deep.
Down?
No waving off these most
mournful messengers
still messengers
sad and stealing
                        (Hush there) – only
not within seeing of the sun.

Resign them,
sign them,
seal them,
send them,
motion them with breath.

Whatever's prized and passes of us,
everything that's fresh and
fast flying of us,
seems to us sweet of us,

and swiftly away with,
done away with,
undone.

So beginning,
be beginning to despair.
O there's none, no no there's none:
with sighs soaring,
soaring sighs deliver.
Them:
      Beauty-in-the-ghost.

All Sing

Three biters bitten:
Earth's eye. Earth's tongue. Earth's heart.
Our counterparts cleaved. Wreathed. Cloven.
This age and era's evil ills
dearly and dangerously sweet
delights buried deep.
Tell us where?
A wild web.
A wondrous robe.
Tell us where
our lungs must draw and draw
a hair
an eyelash
a care kept.
Where kept?
Where?
Tell us where?

Around the beating heart.
In the fine flood.
In the deathdance in the blood.

Annexation

Gaol Song – Part 1

No physics
can explain
the tortured ball of
mind screwed up and
savaged into dense primordial
blacK
      Holes obliterate
inscape
remembered stars
and home-hills filled
with mists
          seep through
the impenetrable walls
again
     and again
to stain
      with damp
and wordless weepingS

Gaol Song – Part 2

picking out what isn't said
between the teething lines and
blocked out crevices
                fingers bleed behind
scuffed words
                barely nailed
hands
                scratch and trace
the mortar silenced stone
                 quarried in that chink
                 of three lettered light
sandwiched by preponderant absence

Gaol Song – Part 3

No messages allowed.
Triggers & cues
plot holes
to fill with dynamite
blow bleeding syntactical
structures to smithereens
(significant harm)

with bluff
hysteria glowed
blooded
in raw red nights of
panic police
where (incubated and bred)
public imagination grows
a law unto itself
unknown
it ritualises abuse

shakes the
dormant ghosts
awake and startling

Gaol Song – Part 4

sneak-reading
(under crosses)
search light search
block-outs
lift-offs
ever between
slipped extremes
  squashed i
    n sidewiz
       glm
    ps   st
      t
    ouch
forbidden meets

              (the lunatic guilt swings)
    blinded
  we pin the tail
  in the donkey's
    eye

Speech-Snatchers

STRIP SEARCH

Stripping off the signifieds.   Metaphors.
The mumbo jumbo prance from sound to seemingness.
Confined.   Inturn the words.   Boxed.   In.
This space sucks speech-magic.   Interns.
Usurps control.   Cuts.   The Arch and Gaffing
Lords misrule and twist
                    the flickering night to
                            flickering day
smudging twilight dumb across
                    abandoned screams.
            That never-thought possible.

Blind Talk

      we only believe
     your truth telling
         it like we
          want to
     hear what we
        don't is

                                                               lying

          through
       your yellow
           rotten
            teeth

lying

         dangling
         ont end
            of
             s
             t
             r
             i
             n
             g
             s
            of
           root
        twisted
           FIBS

Material Evidence

immaculate black　　　　　　(iron slam butchering daylight
gowns fair sneer
snort　　　　　　　　　　　　(ruptured beast
sort of
woosh with well
– booper well –
heeled being　　　　　　　　 (jibber stag

righteousness hangs smart　　 (swineswill
each stinging fold
grin-crease　　　　　　　　　(disfigured beneath crowns
cheesed with pampered hands
　　　　　　　　stainless
pulling ropes with the
quick fingered quick
of weavers　　　　　　　　　 (weeping weeds

quality abounds
profoundly balanced
textile:
time honoured weft
warped infallibility　　　　　　(textured and terrorised

SWEET TALK

'stop bleeding on our walls'
our pre
judicial quest
is staggering to
out
and knock the silly
wanted word   (one teeny-weeny)

spell bastard cant you?
sign a
cross our
bleeding hearts
desired
drip   (one softly-softly drop)

weep stupid cunt you?
one inky indelible blub
once creamed-off drop of bloodshadow
one magic mark
of tellingtale
stigmatic
guilt   (one ticklish touch)

Confiteor

    lips crinkle   :   sickeningly part
              reptilian
             sloth-words
                crawl
                 slow
                  lee
           from corners
            dribbling
            creatures
         crushed t'warm
           thick juices
                 a
         pool of bleat
     a bleed of double talk
     ever redding torment
   sprouting wound-words
       word-insects
            rooted
               in
             throats
            guzzling
             lament

Playtime

fistfuls of revenge   (we let rip
torn
routed out   (tear away the hairy
most grievously
screwed to poppies   (to pinky point
straddled exceedingly
in thoughtword in deedy
exceedingly   (behind
through your fault
through your fault   (closed doors
through your
most grievous fault-face   (systems echo
at at at
window grill
dripping   (spilling towers
gun-games
needlework   (strewn

Out-thoughts

... *of* CHATTOX ...

As the hill imperceptibly steepened
and dimmed
the invisible squadrons
multiplied to
fever
pitch beating
deep and
crammed
against themselves and each
pitched
at the plagued
inner roof of my skull
browning
bruised with the spray
of ceaseless distress
trying to
out
to be aired and wing-ing
(it is the way of words –
to leave yet
to remain:
to breed in
absence:
in the immaculate
space of decay.

So my name
became
my curse (or vice versa
it doesn't really matter:
egg-chicken-chicken-egg-chickadee-
chickabiddy-biddychatter-chatterbox-
Chattox-

Chatter shivered
from my toothless mouth
and thin
senior citizen lips –
each word
(as is their way –
elbowing its turn
to shine and
astonish.

But only I was amazed
by my outbreaks of
quirky
metaphors and
unchallengeable leaps to
lucidity
at invention that beggared
hypocrisy
and most of all
at how my mind
could fold in on a
pure
unstressed monotone of
silence
when all around me
raged.

. . . of DEMDIKE . . .

My pictures of clay:
They were my art.
Not the pitch and toss of play or
Sunday pleasure painting
but the teasing of spirit into the
dumb foxed earth.

It was the best and finest art
(a speedy way to make or take a life)
I spiked it with droplets of wonder
to be drunk unwittingly by children
and bring small animals to rest . . .

. . . the crest of my days . . . my life . . .
solitary moments . . . by the banks of the
Ribble and Calder I sat me down and chuckled
and sometimes wept . . . but mostly screwed up
my face into balls of exquisite contentment.

Oh certainly the images cried.
It is the way of clay.
Wetness . . . oozing through fingers . . .
make-believe eyes running . . .
to the far-off alarm call of birds.

I dried them. Fixed them. Thornpricked them.
Then sat well back and waited for the
diabolical climate to heighten.
Obliterate.

. . . *of* ALICE . . .

Flapping wildly in
cloud broods
move and roost of hill rain
I never tired of.

Getting high caught
in mist-loops
steering my determined straight on
into unchoreographed circles
and the confused same spot.

White. Sightless. Bafflement.
Thickening animal throats
mutating child   man   woman
and the half-faced apparitions
stained sliver of eye
meeting sliver of I in
the glare of mutual suddenness.

And when it lifted?
It gathered excuse and
withdrew my license for the
welling-up of unspeakable wow!
Consorting with elements:
fractious, undesirable,
contra, alive. The pit

against pit of rootless
ease. The feed for my ungovernable
core to help me fight the regime of
mealtimes and the stifling niceties
inbetween –
called 'life'.

. . . *of* 'MOULDHEELS' . . .

I swear
folk dropped dead either side
of curse – they have a tendency to –
we didn't invent mortality
death came regardless
but the mind slavers – turns cannibal –
chance is connected – devoured
throats hurt – constrict
the inflamed lump of raw foresight –
swallow and keck
swallow and keck
keck.

Unfussed as always the
dead bled fresh blood –
I swear
they needed no encouragement from us –
willingly – with gasp
the shrieking and the
foul yelling
sucked out
long
at last

. . . of ANNE . . .

strange things in earth be
came familiar –
figments honeycombed
actualised
         sized up shockingly
without warning –
these things noisily alonged
vibrantly existed

membranes stranger
squatted – flared viral
– acuity mangled senses –
squatted and smeared through under
growth breathing visibly. audibly. ir
regular. wiped glutinous cells against
naked ankles – nerve contractions –
– revulsion –

families starved into strange creatures
– otherworld animals –
eyelids sloughed and twitched for comfort
for food and fire
for quench

retina burnouts
the scorch of contagious dreamscapes
parallel nightmares
beloved anaesthetic.

. . . *of* THE BULLOCKS . . .

squeezing through gaps
of hurt and backbreak
we travelled for miles –
   pressured by ripeness
          by furious blood

       (no genteel tittering lark
        puckering lips to an Ooo-o-o-o)

    GREAT GOBBY SPURTS OF WIDE OPEN

nagging at the hill
and hanging valleys
daft-mad with root spikes
& spirits
     piked with
feeling tangents

      TILL WE CRIED

. . . of SQUINTIN LIZZIE . . .

No, I was no beauty that's true
but with each telling my ugliness grows
like a bodily fungus
and guilt spreads accordingly
as though the two were somehow related.

How far has it spread now?
That my one dimensional
irreversible eye
could griddle spit at ten paces;
that no feckless speck of grit
daring to lodge in its deep
deformed corner could
hope to bring up a tear
or wipe away its malevolent glint.

And its counterpoint forming the unhappy alliance?
Cast in its asymmetrical role
roving over bodies, unrepentant,
turning stars and stomachs, throwing up
fear upon aesthetic fear;
an obvious pool of iniquity.

Still, you've got to laugh, in fact,
in the twisted face of such poppycock
I could easily break into a cackle –
but I think the irony would allude you.

. . . of ALIZON . . .

Sure we dreamt charms:
stared into watery space making
ripples across the boredom
and piss-thin broth

and those sometimes dry summers
sinking head-low and happy in
grasses and bracken:
mating with ghosts.

Sure we made spells:
knees under chins toes wiggling
fingers doing silly dances knotting
hair in kiss curls

to the tock-a-tock mechanicals of stars
swopping giggle-gossip and riddles
till rain spat and scattered us
back to predictability.

. . . *of* JAMES . . .

A weary life.
Vacancy sod.   Perpetual damp.
Our very entrails fusted.   Swoll.
And the nights: Dead blue they goes.   Lurid-like.
Glowy cold.   Starved to each
poriferous bone.   Aching warmth.   Aching
feet creepin up between Alliz inner thighs screamin
gedoffsob-laughin little Jenny joininin
flailin daft-to-bleedin kicks
six seggy eels scouring dark
for blood heated landings and mother
groanin shudup moanin grow up please
to her self-soft sleep and earth warm dirt
of her dreams –
as thirty little piggies
squealed demented –
in extremis.

... *of* JENNET ...

Fish-damp creepy-green
                weirdy world   ghost ridden
I-ever drumming
                I-daring mouths to open to
                              s-t-r-e-t-c-h
painted faces to cracking point
                across X-roads

(the rolling dream hills
                murmured to the north)
masked dancer of night
                s u n b l e d
taunter   taunted
flayer of shadows
        cock walker
                s t r u t t e r
darting heavy spit
infecting the abysmal night
                time killer
                skin hoverer
begin the tongue twist inquest

(the rivers lisped unfunnily)

That giggle-game trickled to the brink
we re-formed
        ganged
        crawled on all fours

laughing at granny
sucking on her bad eggs

me and Jamie: seeds alert:
playing at animals again.

. . . of ALL . . .

Wish-burnt to bone:
To out-think. Out-manoeuvre.
Out-last you.
To move. Shapeshift. Move again.
To conjure your breakdown.
Seizure.
Wish energy govern our strategy.
Stand the brunt of our own impetus.
Absorb our own momentum.
To turn every key   Learn every combination.
Every take-down. Pinning.
Escape reversal.

We will we will split your will.
Pit our every muscle against every yours.
Shadow box.
Soft-sole and side-kick.
Steal
up behind you
tap
(so gently)
tap   tap
your left shoulder
ghosting   you won't see   standing right
tap again
(in opposition)
ghost double   see us not
again.

But you'll know we are there.
Know it is us.
Breathing.
Waiting.

We studied the back of your head and shoulders.
They were not beautiful.   Not even vulgar.
They were closed and peevish.
How could such mediocrity of form
block our forward charge.   Damn our flow.
Cease celebration.

We wished out.   Just to pass.
Please.   We said it nice.   But no.   Fear showed
through. Had to.   Finally.   Run a finger down
your spine.   Feathery.   Teasing.
You turned.   You faced us.
We turned.   We faced you.
Your mouth turned up.
Ours turned down.

The Replies

ANNE WHITTLE REPLIES

a deal more
crafty than
uz
they knew
things never
uttered
in words
arms length and
longer than a
think
thi med id up
with things never
born
till pushed and named
from their gobs
lying
withershins
they knotted uz proper
in tittle-tattle
&
chains

*

straight up they
crawled
between our brain-curls
and
pin-winkled out
ower
tight black slugs of
monosyllables

Elizabeth Southern Replies

Unification creates power.   Creates remains.
Unification creates exclusion.   Persecution.
Random cells need violence
to club and hang together –
        hang together!   Ha!
Bloody comics in
great bonds of fear –
hate-baiting coagulated fear.

Their movement formed
our position.
We slid to the edge
without heaving
or flutter. Without motion or commotion.
We hadn't the learning
to read us right.

We hadn't the food
for big-boned words to
kick mule-like
the wisest fool.

The switch was on.
Our world span:
The centrifuge of
virulent plasma clotted
huddled.   detached.
and made us
thin pale
        we
running down our
sparrow-boned
        legs.

ALICE NUTTER REPLIES

Alice through the centuries
of unrecorded silence.
That is my story:

Your bedtime night-night
fairy tales fill
cells
with injury
hurt the heart and
bleed the kick from
words
hanging limp from my
lips
those perfectly wrought
curlicues of sentences
dripped to my feet.

Sound spirited away.   Unwrit
forever
my inconvenient reasoning
my one stab at life
cut. . . .

Katherine Hewit Replies

It hurt.   Being
felled by a blunt brain.
A nincompoop
pokin iz nosey
wi manicured nails
tapered to cynical infinity:
Pin pointy dead onz.
Ten witherin sticks to taunt.

E was nowt budda Jimmy-bum-licker.
E lived down't lane in a big owse
wi iz porky fatted fingers drippin
rings and blottin copy
after nervous copy – and for what?
A right royal smile?
The patronising smirk of
ultimate noble birth to charm iz drab
and impotent circle.

A could ave pushed iz super up
for't grief and sufferin e set in motion
and time trapped eternity,
A could ave done a lot o things – hypothetically –
with water mirrors and half moons A could ave
gagged the snotty little bugger
talkin down iz nose
talkin do-dah-lah-di like
talking do-dah-lah-di

ANNE REDFEARN REPLIES

I remember my name
wafting like autumn
through the corridors of stone
and the occasional little pocket
of clarity.

It came curling round my body
securer with every repeated utterance
its fronds caressing with familiarity
constricting with unshakeable belonging.

Redfearn. So sticky.   So brightly mine.
Until the book pressed shut.
Pressed out the light.
Dried up the sap.
And I vanished at the wave
of the nametakers.

Jane Bulcock & John Bulcock Reply

Between the sigh and the relief
the floor caved
and we danced on air
prematurely
the river was not human,
northern clouds were stuffed
with hills and mountains,
the mother's son
the son's mother still.

Between the Not and the Guilty
they switched the rules
so anyone
could swing along to
none sense
and separate the same
the related
at will
– a giftie bunch –
we handed em that
– a bunch o' bastards –
we handed em that an
all
the fat earth wobbled
on its imaginary
axis.

ELZABETH DEVICE REPLIES

Your nightmares spilled over
and sucked me in.
Couldn't wake you.
No, couldn't wake myself but
the dead stirred slightly
on the third scream
and the days became dark
without centre
of sense.

One visit
to this reality
has been enough for me
with its ways and means
of making us
chalk words of desperation before
smashing the slate
clean into the face of
oncoming
dawns and all my born dreary days to this
ever nearing death of
laughable proportions.
This trumped up charge of nothing
to nowhere
but your fantasies of flight
and ugly imaginings.

ALIZON DEVICE REPLIES

I just dwindled into the situation
      dwindled into life really
what alternative?
fourteen and female – an unloved combination

violence seemed futile
to smash the head and
             fists
against an anger
        a dungeon wall
bloodies only the moment
        and yourself

a transient relief? – not really –
an exchange of pain? – not even that –
distraction
pure distraction

the situation still surrounds
reinforced – immovable
            manacled
still there
the prating coxcombs
                soft-brained rulers
indifferent nature
          cynical history

ARE YOU LISTENING?
I said
I just dwindled in . . .
till late August . . .
shut my weary red-rimmed eyes . . .
dwindled out . . .

James Device Replies

I wasn't here   I was here   I won't
here I wasn't   here I was   here I
wasn't' was
here
     today   gone   to
fora feeble
        bit part
               my tongue off on
                      off was was not
     here was I was not I t-here I was here me
HEAR ME
w-here was   why was
they was draggin me
to won't here along
        to wasn't here my
                 part bit
     snip-snippity
          my strut kicked feeble
tongue lollery
     lip-s-titched to-g
buggered and frog marcht t t-here
     w-here I was not
        HEARD

All Reply

What was that jingle?
'Now the book is open spread
Now the writing must be read
Which condemns'
What did it mean?

The impenetrable is impenetrable
until penetrated:
the mind could not grasp this
but
the gentle downrush of a sigh
the (transfixing) power of pain
the absolute (   ) ness of pain
this
it could grasp:
as memory became moment became memory
and the mouth opened wide with a shuddering
with a split / dawn / realisation
damming the vastness –
        utterness
      out and outness
        speechutter
        word chains
the mind could not
    can not bear
it slidslides back into trivia:
imbecilic elation.

Just ad(d) jingle.

Touching the Everywhere

THE ETERNAL BEWILDERMENT OF JENNET DEVICE

I weird sang.   High trilled and skirled.
I led a merry crab dance.   Bright.
Kookie-mad.
Rhymed thing with thing string . . .
word buntings.   Wildways
across XXXXXXXXXXXX
For ever acting.   Playing.
      all   out

OH MA
mi maa   mi mother
mUth   er   ing
muth   rin
muR   ther   ing   ringa
killything-a.   Gran.   Ali.   J.
killyall thing-s bright XXXXXXXXXX
killymaa
killykin a killy killy kin
ever mother mothering (eat yer din dins)

O mother mine
mother o me
mother o diva
mother o prima-diva-donna on
the hill-sang
Mother-O   Me-O
O
that lime lit cherry glow
moment
table high and turning
mi heart content. . . .

a turn of consequence unknown

till
slow and sinking in
till
known out loud

alone

OH MA
the word all round
is

TOUCHED

Trilogy

La Tormenta

(With plundering from The Tempest*)*

Heat that Feb ice. Spell melt.
T'wild frozen waters in that
ittered sky pelt downd
sunless pitch
jagged – it pricks the
soft cheeky brains.   Afeard minds.

S'long Inglaterra. S'long Orchard Square.
Us runaway names listing wreckerlessly
t'be cast stoneyed taxiing down
the airy all ways of eternity.

Upslung at last orgasmic gasp
hook off nerves
stripped bare eyes
leaking resinous pollen.
Crying:
What! Must our mouths be cold?

(you are young you said
you must enjoy your
self who died beyond the
nine lives
of cats)

> ***Sprit guide riding high. Mischef meker.***

Not half-drunk enough. Not half-love.
Even when an hourish later
paprika earth hit us at half-slant
dazzling unexpect of spice
heating hot

appalling hungers for
everything but food

Cravedaze. Not half.
Half-nod cut. Enough.
Rubbed crimpt eyelids
seez duty freez vanish.
Who put wild water in this roar?

An unsettled fancy is upon us.
An unwrit score rewrit.
'Fasten your seat belts' says Bette,
at the foot of the bumpy stair.

With flickt wrist
t'heavens
ope'd.

Sonic bullroarers
neckstretchers
stampeders on the wing
shaking living daylights
oust our dreading bones.

                         Toss't dice. Yinegar.

Fly blowed. Hoisted.
D Day One.   Godlost.
We split we spit farewell!

(tricksy spirits were abroad)

Down
and slumped in
sting of godglitz

weighted with static
collective
thankingyee sighs
tongue tips kiss
grit and tracery of dog
shit soft staining drinks
stick-a-lips – cling film – clung
filigree of dead skin
glitter dust fag ash
cheek to check a
signature of some body's blood
drip-written on pave stones.

Foreign forest floor.
                terror terra firma
                              WONDEROUS HEAVY.

Landlocked

In this cloud-capped city
some will lose fear of
violent fragrance and all things gold
by accident most strange in
flamed amazement: sometimes we'd divide
and burn in many places.
Bars. Backstreet grooves. Esquinas.
Lying plazas. Round squares.
Rare wantings. Melancholy daemons.

Duende's all the raging

Crike in the open-mouthed night
no(t)ches glass gem
bled red gaps I lost one rapid

drift along the length of my body
it dripped from my ring
shoosh . . . shoosh. . . . shoosh
slow
as
rose
hip
syrup.

Red bleddings

teeth sink in
Toledo
Chinchón
chin-chin chin-chin chin-ch-
in
deeply seedy bikers
bar the music of
pomegranates
anchovies
well oiled fish
slivers.

We cannot believe
our very-eyes oh yes our
very-eyes we cannot believe
Sopa Goyesca La quinta
creps del sordo
vegetal in season
and what has
Tarta comtessa
got in store
topped only
by an earthenware owl

Gauze-flutter of curtains
spook the white room dumb
blanca deep dancing
these bangled wings and
rusty swords in the

       dead of corridors

such stuff as dreams are made of . . .
rabid sadtoned arabesques . . .
hip sways . . .
death riffs. . . .
brave new heart-beats

       chin-chin chin-chin chin-chin
         chin-chin chin-chin chin
           chin-chin chin-chin
             chin-chin chin
               chin-chin
                 chin
                  ch

Prague Spring

When the Russians rolled in I
was selling papers to
agents and
Alexander Dubček
became a name to pronounce

Broadsides not quite the length of Wenceslas
Square dripped tanks off the edges anon
my sixteenth birthday
I catched the
grainy grey images
of a-dying people
and put them in my pocket
the way you do with falling stars

In a Prague spring of thirty years later
I stumbled off the beaten track
narrowly not killed on Petřin
hill the night they burnt witches over
the river for
being women and missing
the mirror maze totally

To land was not to fly but scamper and
burrow through the undergrowth trying
to find the after-curfew lights and
fast food is sure as sure a
cruel oxymoron to the lost
longing soul and hungry

Over the river there is
always the other side of the river where
Princess Libuše gathers a single mushroom
sighing heavy with visions:
the god warriors will come a-godding
a-good king will bury his hatchet
in the holy rood
Vitus will fling
and five days after Agnes
is sainted
the velvet revolution   begins

Darkly clever jokes fill darker
pubs at weedle-ends glacé cherryful eyes
stain-cults of fine bohemian isinglass
intensely lumes from nooks
older than digged up roman teeth.
– *it wasn't a million years ago miners used fishskins*
for light in tin mines in-ingland –
but if Chamberlain sold them down
the river a
a more beautiful
    river is
hard to be sold down

Down the cellar the dregs still
left: the overstayed
falling
dreamily with love:
two soft speaking men
knives and bright forks
thick blackbent tablesunder
stiffstarch whitestuff
and us with us under
flamewick spell.

From three bears to
white ox in a matter of
centuries the floor
length apron opened
and underhanded the
samizdat menu:
'*Giant Mountain cabbage soup*'
'*Game from our Meads and Copses*'

With squat poppy-out eyes the
medieval denim-clad sword swallower
unswallowed then rammed two six inch
nails up his nostrils for dessert putting
one off our pudding and one
off our dumplings but neither off our
BECHEROVKA which kicks
stomach pit spreading
molten with herby-ore
ace primer for the
land of lurid fairytales

(Golem Watch)

What is Golem?

Artificial-man made-clay
Servant-savant
Key fig o magikyl Praha
un
finisht
coarse
lopt

How did Golem look like?

Drest asa shammes
mythical mudman
tall puft features
hal-met-like hair-heavy
buskin shoes
jacket pressed parchment
like a jazerant
      like armour padded cotton hardened
          in salt water astec warriors
               wore
                  war-h

How does one make a Golem?

  One must purify oneself then
  one forms a pup
            pet from vir
                    gin earth and
walks it

```
    in a cir
              cle while
re
        citing
the letters of the tet
                ra
                gram
```

IN FOUR HUNDRED AND SIX (SIC)
PER
MUTATIONS

How make Golem move?

One writes the word EMIT
                    (truth)
sharp on its forehed *(sic)*
or places the SHEM in his mouth

How does one the Golem destroy?

By walking it in a circle in the op
po direction while reciting alpha
bet backwards as a curseplaying close
attentions to the number of turns
the combinations of
lettersand
the way one walks

  and the way one walks
        one walks

(The Last Day)

On the way to **Kutná Hora**
we met a lonely man
a loney man we met there
he was a **Russ-i-an**
  On taking of his photo
  our fate snapped in his hands
  disappearing out the blue
  blaze offa the earth face
  he stole our lacy plague-bothered bones
    Oh unseen ossuary built on the back
    of a half blind monk
    30,000 bodies ram-racked
    and shackled in a death dance
    of monstrances urns and chandeliers
      Our last chance day
      fractured with your flight &
      splinter
      grewing eye-sockets
      wide as saucer dogs
      filling up wi-watery question
      marks drip
      Oh where Oh where did our Russ-i-an gone
        In the **Hotel Europa** life goes
        with a slowhand peeling
        paints seen betterdays
        worsen
        the **C**ola**M**a**c**American**A** brays
        its ways across the oblong
        squaring
        he-haw yea-haa aw gaud

y
cheap perfume bottles
glister with
peacocks and
petals
fall backwards on the
blackened
statues
hulked histories
volute in their
see-through
STONE-LODESTAR

Prelude V

The moment the pin pricked Venice
the Bridge of Sighs
              answered
number one
        across
the quick
Gondolier
          cascaded
down the cryptic
Rialto
    drew
first blood
on University
          Challenge Don't
Look Now
        peered
out the Tee Voo
through morning mists
and western portentous
voodoo
blinds shuttered sight
seeing
cross connections
snaking round our anklets
for snake forms also part of
everything
in   this
   s
  link
    y

I stood in Sheffield on the Building Sites
A navvy and a nutter on each hand
Part actors rising from their rubbled souls
Italiano-tyke bellowed without
end Or elegance Or diphthong
BonJorno BonJorno MoltoBeLLA
bellowed with conspiratorial glee
a noise-filled pause from
neo-classical concrete.
Breeze-blocked.

Swoop in two J's
and don't say
'Venice is rubbishy'
as Claude slayed Rome
but solely praised only
fish market:
of a city built of staggering
beauty on bracken
the fish must have been
unearthily spectacular

We fly on Halloween
nocturnal revel
              destinies
borne down by evidences
over the Alps half
              a
year to the
day
Walpurgisnacht
unwittingly our wedding
eve driven
passion

for
lilies
snow whitened
witch sab
mountains

Faustus
in whim for wheeze
announces
sensation creation in Venice
courtesy of devil-aid
lifted sheer from
Piazza to Pointless
on Satan's stickle back
haunches –
but brutto-face lets him fall
    a   a
     r   r
       i   i
         a   a
he Faustus hee
nearly gives
up his ghast

'When people propitiated their gods
they stereotyped the limits of their minds'

All in a flitter
dwarf clib-clobs the
calles
hoofin
initsitsybitty
P.V.C. redderhooded
rainmares
dousing the soothsayers

with convulsions and
blindeyed
doubters

e mio marito non can swim
floats in cyberspace
with ease without life
belt wrapped
around
where my arms
wrap around –
physical to abstraction

Whilst Byron stood
number 1
        across
the 4th canto
I randomly opened the page:
'to separate contemplation'
it stops me in my flow of
webbings against the naggering backdrip
of monomaniacal rains and flu
– I need oil-skin – nurofen –
we'll all Autumn '98 need
well-connected toes like
mother's born before
they cut them.   Cut them?

Anti-amphibian disformists!

No sooner gone than back flips
a postcard from Zennor
and reckons once
        across
a time
a mermaid married and

merried to atone to a
sweet tone of +cultural divides
and separate contemplation

So Mary born before my time –
as mothers tend to be –
uncut-aquatic   water-babe
wimmerswims upstream >>>>
from Lido to Piazzale Roma
beating Byron flappers down.
But we just KoKo'd jumped the
Vaporetto
feet dry 'n' cosy down its
Grand
S
Kaly
S
pinebone

Hit one more nail
in the kitch wall
to hang suspension~~~~
the hand that sent Zennor
daubed Adriatic reds
and oily sets of
sun bloods and oranges
and even as it dries
cool Canaletto comes to York
undaunted by its 'Micklegate Run'
notorious
he stashes the entire
Grand Canal under his
carnival cloak –

quivering angelica in aspic

– still falls the rain
on England &
Wales
turns to rivers and ruins and
each house will
build a shipshape
makeshift gondola
and it will cost us
all nothing at all
to sail to Clapham Common
or Wherever
and why go to Venice
when Venice comes to us
at the drop of its name
in a ceaseless drip . . .

Manufractured Moon

(Subject: Fox barks)

Sat upright and owl-eyed for hours so thoughts got to pellets & droppings of words but to longhand e-mail or fax foxes barking trees weeping their sticky in the early hours flashing sodium tales in the techno light show of all night club fang.

City animals on their eternal nocturnal party rounds. A fox is burying meat pies in the pitch dark of a first division football feud. Dive, dribble and chip in the centre. They will hunt and bray it down the four lanes and dual carriageways of the ringing roads. Wild life and night birds cluster round the heart of metropolitan hip-hop-scotch. Farmer farmer may I cross your golden river . . .
game from the streets.

Dawn will finally break me into the land of nod and off I go like yesterday a man got shot two streets away.
Come up and see
me sometime.
Getha

(Subject: Hungered and Loafing)

Fresh air in my city lights. I breathe soft sofas of joy. I cross off the calendar days. I cross them backwards. They meet the ones coming forward and halve the time. To halve and to hold . . . to have your cake . . . and yours such a rich home-made. Was Sara Lee a gypsy?

My calendar is tucked in a fright in the corner of intricate plastic lace. It's offish white. The Last Supper of 2000. Pale lilac wall weeps through its lacy pores. Christ. He holds a heart shaped cob against his breast. The positioning is just so. Under the matching lilac-shaded standard lamp the room's a tip with shadow. Lopsided. All the apostles are men.
Getha

(Subject: Various Sirens. Choppers)

Urban suburban and every damn half rhyme. T'night's'like soundtrack to climaxing film of Vietnam. Choppers joy riding galore. Chasing kids. Not a meek mewling lamb in sight. Dirty maelstrom low throat laugh. Multidirectional mono. Mean. I mean I feel so Friday night the furniture just sweats perfume, booze and half remembered sex. Oodle, canoodle me home a lone rangeress with untouched skin and sober as a barristocrat. Farmer-Farmer may we cross your golden river to take our father's dinner . . . look forward to seeing you big
                              bad outside world
meets faux-mad Arcadia Must dash –
Getha

(Subject: Stone Laugh)

I toy with words and twist the twisty bits of my hair 'exhibits in an inhibition' this almost sentence reoccurs without warning. What does does mean? A priceless pot on a shy rickety table. I stick my life out. I'll play divertimentos and make maps of the face of my cheeky-chops bare-breasted goddess. Such laughingly love at first sight should not go uncharted. The moment in the mind fleshed out. Hiding from seek – in the eye-level sun – in the blazing embarrassment – in the face of the back of the church – in the village – in the graveyard – in the strange little county called Rutland.

Now I'm not too sure all the apostles are men. One seems too beardless and fine jawed.

Farmer Dark-Force may we par take our father's boiled dinner as it is in heaven?

This is an ever and it's lasting.
Getha.

(Subject: Falling Outs)

The blind even quivered at the iddy girl tungsten thin and burning bright fell out with all gods in a big way such as only young-age can with starry id. They conjured miniature animals for warfare but they readily scorched and rebelled.

The lambs a-lit.
>   Its face turned a shiny teaspoon to the
>   west beam that was.

Always always,
Getha.

(Subject: Breakers)

All at sea in the city.
This ash I wandered streets and turned at every café bar. Flew flew flew. My shoulders creaked with monkey and the blustery and my guardian angel a-beating my head hair to a tarnished knot. Puzzle snarled. I felt in my pocket for my tissue and pricked my finger on a cocktail stick shaped like a sword for sticky of cherries. Intending to strike at the heart of torment I picked out a lovers lock and a chunk of Irish Sea. My first concerto is in the making. It has no spots. It may yet be amphibian.

May it cross your golden river? Dark-Force Fisherman.
Getha

(Subject: Rogue Rage)

All the apostles are men but one is without a beard and leaning too willowy to Christ. Is this a trick of plastic lace? A sleight of oversight? He looks on close a she. Joan of Arc jumping icon banks, sabotaging sacred narratives. The last immovable tableau. Fire I fear will follow.
I fear also I note by night my sentences ring oddly and raw and now the day draws as I do ... all in ... I will cease to speak as I don't want to startle the birds from sleep. Where *do* birds sleep?
Getha

(Subject: Radio. Gales. Floods.)

What's that you say. Another great escape ... life's an eternal fencing match ... keep inoutin ... shake ma ma nature an all that jazz ... hips in the offing. Can Aliens make the breakthrough? My day after day is backgrounded with radio-pulp. Flat above is endless Jungle. What a jiggersaw. What is a jiggersaw? As yet no flood or trickle of luck with work ... check ads and sads and sod em all maybe I'll robabank and Bonnie it without Clyde across the world. Farmer-Farmer. The apostle is suspiciously perfumed.
Joan of Arc is on hold.
Getha.

(Subject: Discovery)

I'm faxing a map of Jupiter. I'm worried about the hot spot. The new flash points are now called 'reports' as a soothing strategy for public panic. But study the map if you please. The red seems sulky. Not quite how red should act. My friend is close but colour blind. He cannot throw light. He eats green strawberries. Purple doesn't exist. He weeps for wimberries all through the season. To him the red spot's a kiwi. I think he's obsessed with fruit. Maybe he's right. Maybe strawberries glow with envy. Traffic lights make him hungry not angry. But tell me about the hot spot. Is it out of sorts. May we cross its golden river. Our father's dinner is
growing cold.
Be cool Be.
Getha.

(Subject: Amber Alert)

Hell-p!
And as I write a stranger is flickering under the leaning street-lamp. Out the window. I wish he would choose another. This afternoon an unseasonable heaviness of air. The city restless with shifting signs. Rubbing undercurrents. Jumping lights. Pedestrians stage-diving pelicans. Jaywalkers. Ill-mannered starlings. A subdued iridescence on the necks of lame pigeons. Discoloured glister of penniless window-shoppers. Oldsters cheesed.
A daylight moon thoroughly fed-up all round.
I wish he would go.
The flickering man.
Write soon
Getha

(Subject: Din. Neuralgic Ringings)

Did you reply? Computer curdled then crashed to obliv. Living here is neither here. Things closing in and amazing facts curl up their toes. I lean out the window crooning. All whole roads are up. Diversions to nowhere everywhere. Heads ache with pneumatic drills. When they found the frozen mammoth it still had buttercups in its mouth. Still edible. Floral steaks. It's a time thing. All day industrial rock . . . all powered by . . . tax . . . my notwork neuralgia . . . dust bowls of thinks . . . are Oman and Yemen female landscape . . . curvy dunes sucked dry . . . strangled gardens . . . Babylon . . . pollution . . . the Americans have just bought God.
Pandemonium is the word of the day. Let us pray.
P A N D E M O N I U M A M E N

Getha

(Subject: Sodden)

Walls grin wetly. And HE's there again.
Up to his knees.
   Newspaper in hand under
      the sodium ghastly.
The apostle is moving.
Do I
not that
like
Get . . .

(Subject: Back on Track)

Farmer-Farmer home safe and trying to catch straggling sheep
bleats as they galumph through the whorls of my ears: this
sentence is too long. Don't sheep ever sleep? Eep eyp eyarp. With
eyes to slice a primordial onion. To lie-side-down is-to-die. A
crying shame. Your silhouette on the hill is not a national treas-
ure. Our nation is shrinking and violent. Your golden river. My
father's dinner.
The mill.
Last night this early morn I drove the city streets – so muggy for
so early spring. Drainy glottal stop . . . the window wide after
midnight . . . an amazed mouth . . . conversations, contretemps
tittle-tat hit earshot.

'what the	side eer	.crude.i cry	ingland
stop . .	flame in in	in allin . . .	blonde.bluid.s
y(w)hoo.	in..anas I	yer mind . . .	lost de key . . .
where did .	. . woz . . . wot	ful . . . t	.smol world
over here..	yucol me . . .	throated . . .	big cit . . .
yam sick	leave! it a	a'll throttle	catrut sit e
(Ooh never) . .	sed leave it a	. . . pizza . . .	smelt swerds.
. watch it . . .	lone bol irks	ever let me	. . . .mewl
babe . . .	lukad	hear here	shut out
s/f/luck its	'isthad'the	you say eat or	shout and
bottlemate	moonooerr . .	met al bar	god alof.
. . . s/da(f)t	. don't.be	none . . .	United. Un.
bas-t-ar tara	crule cry	injure . . . n	
see u out 'n'		. . . jalfazi . . .	
out		oys . . . 'zchoo	
		from finglan'	
		no	

I was cruising for cool. Foxy hot footing towards the main shop-
mall. Disquieting shiver of breaking glass breaking as ever some-
where else. I drove through the heart and out the other side.
Vanished. Abracadab. Walls grew massive. Stone bruising stone.
Skyblotters. Humourless Victorian monoliths. Industry work-
ships swaying dirty breath down neck. Bones against ghosts. Ran

through umbilical bridges and archways. Past scrambled. Crashed into newness. Lean reflecting glass. Imported steel. Bouncing light. Loveliness.

I headed home into I.

The apostle sashayed round the last supper a la Rita Hayworth a la laa Gilda. My heart jumped in my mouth with respect. Window boxes grew miniature Edens. The sun some moment will stream. Break into fox-trot round table legs. My heart feels like a host. It sticks to my roof. I take it out and put it about. Leavened wild life everywhere. Gone-to-earth goes up the cry. I need late-night biscuits with salt. Come see me in my urban heaven. Meet flying rats and flagrant saints.

It is quiet now. The apostle is still. Sweet city catnaps before sunrise. Air cleaner and chill fresh. I watch News 24. The Americans have just bought Dawn. Stars beyond the streetlights. I lean out my window to croon. Yes, there he is. An unearthly hour. Ginger shock, lamp-leaning, under the manufractured moon.
G.

The Transparent Ones

The Gathering

(High noon. Mid Summer. Terrace. Round table. High Peaks in the distance. Round robin of low sleepless talk. The Transparent Ones)

And in coming over it overcame. Shad. But blue. But.
But brilliant. Waterskin in Landlock. Shad-skein.
Highblownoon encircled terminal.
Strangesobs. Cottonsoft blood. Pink. Candyfloss.
Balmfloat of stretched perception
Caught on. Celestial snag. Meteorite.
Nearer and nee. O. Orbiting. O Obit.
Catch us black inside.
'Cut us w'all bleed, w'all black inside'
Burnt sugar crystals. Brulee.
Sugarcrab.
Starspangled metastasis.
Ai! Comets come Acrashing.
AssssshhhhHHHhhhush . . .

Mood heightens. Speech plays tig.
Anticlockwise. Cockles tail. Wise. Ululations.
Moodblight. Moonlike drench of cloudcover.
Spirits crowd closer.
Branded collaborators.
The circle grews.
You (you) You (you) You (you)
Cellcreps.
Ringa.

AMOEBIC ENGULFING CLOSENESS

In a wide clean language turquoise is
uncomfortable.
It wafts from the Peaks with a gabbling of
green
and slippery mauve.

Around the table an odd coloured speech.
The one who twitters with
sprouting wings is not a
bird.
So sweet. So stop.
So weep. So weep
                with me
                        all of you.

Across Your Dreams in Pale Battalions Go

        Rebel-woman   outlaw-wise
        halts me by that footfall.
        Is gloom after all a
        shade of hand
        outstretched and
        stargatherings?

M recites
a memory

        Heap me over
        this tremend love-
        strange.
        Piteous.
        Futile thing!

Pauses . . .
Roams..
Continues . . .

        From dank thoughts
        that dangle
        from the sighful
        branchlets of
        my mind.
        Such is : what is to be?

Reflected in
the mirror
she reflects:

        What's the big idea?
        Lip to lip metwine wit
        you in wind-walled palace
        quaffing   quaffing
        The taintless chalice
        is not above suspicion.
        Lucent–weeping
        glooming-robes

        room-globing
        purpureal
        daysprinkt with
        sad magic dust

A turn of
face she reads
the childs
Persephone
        Struct iz whip
        earthsplit down
        and downly in
        very-cold he
        carried

M shivers.
Shifts unease.
        flowers wept
        crops stopt
        leaves turned
        raged-red
        and shed
        everything
        shed

In the deep
midwinter
        Still life.
        Mourning.
        Snow.
        Six glacial
        pomegranate
        setting sun
        seeds.

Bluehound

'nix y'am no-am man-nor-beast save once I sate
life's banquet feast-y-eating my own little words -
stealing their happy away'   *J.T.*

But where
are we going?
And what is
it all about?

        Going
        we are where
        about all it is

Does it really
matter
where's
my friend?

        Matter really it does
        friend my-my
        trying to grasp your wagging
        tale cart-wheeling away
        big-hearted thinks
        force ten laughs
        beltering through
        philosophical doors taking
        flying
        Looby Loo's
        at the ill wind.

It is time
to go now?

        Haul away the
        anchor!
        Your imminent
        Alien State awaits your
        grand entrance,
        Pet, wipe your eyes

        at the
        coming of your
        dazzling
        ufo
        afterlifeboat

So life's
like that?
        Like an ilk love on a gnarled
        hand *in* glove *in* tongue *in*
        cheek *in* stitch *in* time does
        its doing with
        your natter-flack
        questions creating
        ineffable Q systems &
        split infinities

And that is
that?
        Pup-a-luv -
        that is that

Then paste this question mark to the centre of the sun

Cliff Hanger

In the midst
came the end
>Well there you go . . .
>dropped off your perch
>quiet as a mohair scarf . . .
>just like your best dream
>dreamt of . . .

Leaving me
>me-all   a-drift
>all-in a day's work
>with a mouth full
>of unsaids so I'll
>have my sayso now

With glitches
& gremlins
>The computer scanner
>drew a blank
>so no o.k.
>you'll not make it
>to my birthday
>though we both knew
>you wouldn't go
>to the bitter ends of
>your ancestral dig
>into colourful
>meaning
>deeply
>shady crooks
>and songbirds
>hooking
>more than
>even we
>bargained
>for.

convergence
of spookilies

        My do at
        Eckington Hall
        fell through a stone
        's throw from
        Renishaw
        's dragon flies spell
        trancing aerial
        hieroglyphs
        in-non-rhyming
        couplets.

        Japanese
        fancy-fish tail
        us humans to the sharp
        corners of geometric
        ponds blowing
        kisses of life
        poised –

Scaling
the heights

        So here is the
        where the winter list
        and shiver of Christmas
        trees await their moment
        where your old
        man's old man's
        beard & fiddle
        scaled
        carousal singing
        stately gates
        rocking and
        shocking the
        maids and ever

so young Lady
Sitwell with
child-wild
Plantagenet
poet.

Keltic Twilight

Swanz

  Tin throated
  keltic sotto voce
  soothing grubber pants
  o drizzlings.
  Impy-eyed & turned up
  lipping 't-poep-sa-nutter'
  Papa Dub.

Snakerz

  '*Apostasy*'
  he hizzles
  warmly Romewards
  '*Apostasy!*'
  with no remorse
  enstrangling holythrone
  enshrined
  Joh-Pau
  rocks
  his serpent. *Rock*.
  We're talking holy *see*.
  See you lisps the obscene
  usurps

The oracle
shakethz

  ' I saw the aurora in '38'
  (she said we would)
  highlarks & jinxloons
  beaking awesome through the
  bannering ore-glow diagonal
  t'wards the second W.W.
  Alpha es et O.

Tales of
scary
miracles

        Three children of Fatima
        all told were asked
        by her white-robed self
        in the whiter heat of day
        'are you ready to suffer'
        And lo! The Portuguese
        field of vision became a
        landing strip the
        size and bustle of
        Heathrow.

        Truncheoned candles ignite
        both ends the prophesies
        of brightday runaway minds.
        Religious tack is truly cruel
        and the crude sun on its knees
        remains unmoved. Unblooded

        we abs-orbit with Abdul.
        Be mused.   Thinking on
        accuracies of Old Mother
        Shipton.

The oracle
ascends

        '*APOSTASY*'
        liplix again
        with hands down
        eyes
        winnin-grin
        full of guinness

brimmingly
you passes on
your borrowed
flowers
flit
in two my
giggly
palms

Then One Morning

She points her
missy
ring-ripped
no-finger

      'For you.' 'For me?' 'For you.'
      'Really?' 'Rely upon me.
      Living alone in a back-flat.
      Companies of g-howls an g-hosts
      through the nesh nights of aloneness
      I noticed you. For you. Really.'

I read her
words to me
she makes a
covenant

      I will re-yern as a snowflake.
      Be-back as a solitary drop
      in a flurry.
      I will land on the outermost
      tip of a
      nose-end and tickle.
      Trickle & treat
      to evaporate with
      out pain
      or maybe-be the
      one flake that
      breaks the bough
      off-of a certain
      tree.

She reads
my unspoke
love

      Kittywakes whirling.
      'Marry him'
      she yellows at my
      goodbye back
      turned

eyewhites gone daffodil
sheshines and
hurls her voice ceilingward
Upperstraight.
See through.
Oracular.
! Do it ! *Exitstage Flowerless Left*

The Unspeakable Softness of Flesh

Skin Panics.
even my words are ridd~~led.
Sense disappears at every touch.
Ideas dissolve before formulation
(uncertainties sneak around corners)

Aqueous morphine alcohol & fear
confuse all the terminals.
Messages splinter
inter
mutant Gethsemanes of agony.

Betrayal is sexual ~~
illusory beauty exquisite.
Hands join in supplication
hands spread flesh spread
death parted lips do
do drip dreadfully
'your future's all used up'
she husks to the ever swelling strain
of the Pianola spook.

In the grip of rising panic
we watch the solitary unleaf furl ~~
There are moments of relief
in every fiction

so go get the lilies ...
your doppelganger just rode into town
sprouting wings
is not a
bird.
So sweet. So stop.
So weep. So weep
             with me
                     all of you.

Insubstantial Thoughts on the
Transubstantiation of the Text.

Unvocalised (private)

More than meat or drink. Better than stars and water.
Words birthed. Made flesh. Took wing. Horrids
and enormities. Chantcasters. Daubing lunarscapes.

The Lone Reader.
Incommunicado.
Unutterings sucked in silent
body folds.
Unstretched organs.
Sonic un ♦temporal nuances subsistent.
Inflexion depopulated.
Accentuation dis♥embodied.
The
    . (pause) .
                    can be *defiled*.
Rhythm *skpt*. Kip*P*ered
Throat sob ~s ~ caught
breath Θ scored ♠ out

Ob+ scene intimacy.
Spectral static.
Mellifluous streamings.
Conceivings concurrent.

The act of reading inquiet is cerebrally absolute.
Corpus in repose. *Corpus in almost repose-us.*
Eye-orbs fly-wink. *gzz*. Mini zigger-*jit*.
Involuntary fidgets.
Atricky bit: cut-red-cabbage brow.
Tics. Itch-*ay*. Sips. Drags.
Scra-*T*-cha~~ cha~~~ *chaa*.
A semblance of a toe-tap. Maybe*maybe*.
The body taken in to (care)
reflex warden .. beady ..

Authorial origins can be dubious. Shape-

shafter. Changeling. Devious. Chancer.
The authoaxer'"'s stalking ground.
A-(h)all of mirrored personas
    interior dreamtempts
    the terrible start of self-meeting
    other me-s-elfs.
Hinterlands. Outskirts of shadowy. A glimpse
of under.
Unpoliced.
Subcranium.
Nocterrestrial

More than meat or drink. Better than stars and water.

Vocalised (private)

More than meat or drink. Better than stars and water.
Words birthed. Made flesh. Took wing. Horrids
and enormities. Chantcasters. Daubing lunarscapes.

Cabinet readings " ".
    Cabal. Acronym variable.
Amongst friends only. *gsts.*
Givens already known.
Inner sanctums. [ ]
Domestic inanimates hovering.
The quiet page ruffled ~~
words up like sap. Exit with frou-frou ~~
vibrations shimmy the anatomy of skull~~
the architecture of viscera ~~
carnal sweetbreads.

Words birthed. Made flesh.

Curved enunciation. *Shussh. Giraffe shways.*
Naked face expressions. **O**
Un-demon-strative gestures.
Off guard quirks. Gaffs. (A misplaced laugh is not
swotted. Swigged. Wiped on cuff).
Unworried **l o v e s** *Soft Wanderings.*
Conversations punctuate.
Body reclining.
Internal organs curled.
Limbs laxed.
The off-shoot flicker. Psyches. Light on
intimate. Stocking
feet. Foot cramp_. (Uncool dance may come later.
Low-glow performance. Conserve with energy.
Shared murmurs in the wilderness.
Can tumble suddenly to perilous.
Stark doubt of mutterance:
Letric

is a (j)eeled live wire?
Made flesh.
Is it within a hair's breadth or a hare's breath?

Vocalised (public)

> *More than meat or drink. Better than stars and water.*
> *Words birthed. Made flesh. Took wing. Horrids*
> *and enormities. Chantcasters. Daubing lunarscapes.*

Public and *pubic* are too close for typographical comfort.
Spoken so pointed it should be spiked with a double 'k'.
Out in the big wide w. be bold.

The bodied poet
broke on the back of phonemes
and puns within heart-reach
or slightings.
Placed rudely in
temporary cradles of
burnt out kirks. Bright
college rooms. Upon-
a-time shops. Portuguese
secret gardens. Dreary
halls of 'is this all there is'
weariness. Any *shrug* or *wow* aspace
to hold
and be
have. (have.)

The show goes on. . . .
                        Poet as an Exhibition.
Body limited in overdrive:
       upright/ uptaut/double-bent/kathakalic.
Voice exitings:
       inc(h)ants/ warbles/sprechgesang /gutturals.
Nerves:
       edgling up arterials of interior weather maps.
Humours:
       four and growing. Corporeal compass points.
Text-gesturals:
       Rhythm. Ythmm. Timing. Timbre.

The Happening-stance:
    The preposterously loud death-thud of the fledgling
    against the bedroom window.

Max somatic dynamics.
Rod-ram.
Downy.

Took wing.

Poet as an Exhibition
reveals the contours of origin:
gender-age race species height
weight dentistry speech defluct
stam 'r twitch.
Fashioning of image:
    from Armani to Market.
Tracery of accent:
    from Sink to Estuary to Estados Unidos.
It's a matter to hoaxers:
    Is the red panda really
    a real bear and well-red?
Mean-time exposure.
Revelation.
    O alpha in extremis.
Personas decamp.

Body mass is conduit.
Words birthed.
Made flesh.
Stiffening conceits into concretes:
A happy maddening.

Adrenaline rush-hour.
Spinal column working overtime.

Neural overload.
Backache in an occupational hazard.
Bony hangovers.
Invertebrates may not perform.
Performers may slither.

Horrids and enormities

Voca-visu (orientation)

> More than meat or drink. Better than stars and water.
> Words birthed. Made flesh. Took wing. Horrids
> and enormities. Chantcasters. Daubing lunarscapes.

Delivered with ambulation.
Mutability.
Paraphernalia.

To perform is to *in habit* space.
Performance is aggressive occupation of
place. Convolvulaceous. Territorial laundering.
Advancing words beyond jealous boundaries.
Equipping body with armoury. Blooms.
Bloss. Webbings.
Blue plastic mac. Feather boa.
Redriding hooded habit.
Dietrich slink –
acrylic shocking-pinkoid bucket.
Flipt charts. Till rolls. Word drops . . .

other placements demand other strategies:
paint filled eggs
Poundstretcher gadgets
double-decker buses
junk shop bayonets (19th century French)
voiceovertapes
cosmetics
garbs of white
red x scarf
hair skewers -
girlywhirl with deep trans-voice –

sonics from soma gullet – bit of spirits and
ghosts attached. From outer whorls.
Journeying from gut
bacteria loiter intent on

emotional prey to
pounce. Churned flutters of
squirrel monkeys and all things
beloved by owls.
Para-dramatic-melees

Proceedings go viral
hemmed by pert puckish tails.

The ritualistic delineation of space.

Chantcasters.

spell spelleps lleps
Scent spraying. Carnal. Nails upalert.
(Keratin overshoot is **a**rd but **d**ead but **v**ital)
Toes in perpetual isometric desperation
clinging for balance:

a body hanging by its feet.
.t.t.t.t.t.

.t.

Fused Sonics (interaction)

> More than meat or drink. Better than stars and water.
> Words birthed. Made flesh. Took wing. Horrids
> and enormities. Chantcasters. Daubing lunarscapes.

Released from solitary.
Musicians come with-wires attached
ill fitted plugs
miscellaneous black boxes
far too many knobs &
forgotten amps behind their
frosted doors.

The spontaneous moment
needs voice checks ☐

preliminaries
for pure
animal heard
instinctive
voice skirl
tronic synth
sax
callow cello
triangled
we
get **sst**Ruck*ing* a
la bobbin-rack
squa*lib-ab*.
Trio. Duo. So.
Klink-glass. Ash. Lo. Comb O Klish.
Imp. Ro. Synch.
One bod mob rile:
    no one's
    no ones
    accompaniment
at break limit

ceilings lose solidarity
interoctave
nuance
e
long
a
yob-yell of horn
e
e-
xtra terrestrial
cello gets
Jenny-belted
in the switch-back
ground
caving
reed~like

Sonic v Semantic

abstraction of
itterance
meaning
fighting for
dear
squalled in
sownd
un estuary ova
k
not(t)ed
omnivorous
noise-fate

Daubing lunarscapes.

Absent Friends

*From Nether Edge to Nether Stowey: two words four hours
six counties and one astonished heart jolt away.*

Raised lips
maraud
rooms of
repros
with a sob of spinel
and ripe of
hot day lupines.

*Adjacent to a memorial brooch beneath three spikes of hair at
Nether Stowey was a shaded place on a bright September day.*

A bright
to read a leaf
through the sun:
a coot foot
in clear water.

*Unexplained events are not bound by storms coming as they
sometimes do under the bluest of skies.*

Brit-jet brack drift
oceans floored for cent . . . . s
salt dimple a-Whitby with-a
fragile
spark it
drives away serps
with a glint it spit out
evil cockle eye.

*The museum closed I roamed alone and never touched forbidden
'do not . . .' A trust that spines the full exquisite down.*

Gutta percha flinch at
imitation rub
highly
dyed
horn a sap a
merican
vulcanite
cane pale pure
exposing innards of
lockets.

> *Enshrined in glass beneath three spikes of hair I read slow*
> *and clear as the Saturday: I read 'six' divided by 'friends'.*

Heart-broke columns
urning birth
succoured death dates
head in
hands give a fig
froots
weeping wallows
perched atop.

> *Six mourning rings Coleridge willowed to his friends.*
> *Items referred to. Not shown.*

Hope boiled in soda.
15 watery minutes cooks eternity
enamelled at a fro
passing hey to ether
catch a-story oops transparent
fame at laaaa . . .

> *Which six friends to cherish till dust us do*
> *wears a ring of hair and gold and seed pearls?*

Death is a test
on earth
for the living begin
again death
is a test on
earth begin
a same

> Was it a game. They came with rough inscription among
> many snakes wrapped a round long hands and skulls
> 'Love my Memory' one demands and others abstract.

Luck of hair
look at air
lock of her or him
singing chaste to a
rude spread virgin
oiled asa
brilliantined Byzantium quiff
in memoriam
touched to a
trinket drop o tears
opal monmoons.

> Throughout Europe they offered young girls ribbons and
> combs for hair which grows quicker than kidneys.

I have a piece of   (I have
thee   (carved you
here on my heaving   (upon
not unworthy of   (the palms
thy being   (of my
now   (hands

> I wondered through the glass which six friends I could so gift.
> To bequeath in absence of doubt of love or sentimental fondness.

Clasping death
in homecraft perspex
plait of links
in the i
dea of dea
th
twinded into
sorted lengths
from a very common
centre

> Hair-weaving was done on a round table by women. Egyptians
> exchanged hair-balls of love. Mexican girls stored their hair
> combings for burial. Lancastrians and Spaniards pull hair for
> birthdays. It grows after death this stuff that angels
> lust after in the after-garden of woman. Cock? Give
> a good knock. Hen? Start again.

Re
m
em
ber
on me
ceed
re
rings
me
-omb.

That night came up upon our heads. Who were the six?.
The curators were kind beneath the fake albatross. So
kind my bracelet became uneasy. The unravelling of
wraiths and their whims. Upon a painted pause the
custodians of memory offered me wine without miracle .

Fancy hair
moulded to
reliquary
a cherry
urn of sucking stone
to gem out
dated keeper
wedding band
dashing reddish
with a rare
man.

A relaxed space – I check the next day. It is the next
and standing. Sky systems not lost identity. Clear
as the day was Sunday. The museum my own.
Beneath the glass. Ribbed sea-sand.

To flaw or else to
sever so

There were no words to describe.
No 'six'. No 'friends'.
Death a test. An earthly.
Brooch bemocked. Ring a swound.
Never a breeze up-blew.

Notes

La Quinta Del Sordo: Based on Goya's etching 'The Disparates'.

Interregnum: Private memory and public ghosts in the timeless landscape of East Lancashire. Centred around the imprisonment and execution of the Pendle Witches in 1612. The text draws in part on the works and words of Gerard Manley Hopkins, George Fox, The Birmingham Six and Stefan Kiszko.

The Transparent Ones: This work is in memory of and thanks to all the patients I worked with over a period of six and a half years as Creative Writer in a hospice and particularly to the memory of my dear friend Tony.

Cover illustration by Alan Halsey.

www.ingramcontent.com/pod-product-compliance
Lightning Source LLC
Chambersburg PA
CBHW030106170426
43198CB00009B/506